STORIES FROM
SIKH HISTORY
BOOK VI

(Banda Singh Bahadur to Rise of the Sikh)

Kartar Singh
Gurdial Singh Dhillon
Edited by
P.M. McCormack

Hemkunt Press

A-78 Naraina Indl. Area, Phase-I, New Delhi-110028

© Hemkunt Press 1971
Fifteenth Edition 1995

ISBN 81-7010-176-X

ISBN 81-7010-176-X

In this series

Book I (Guru Nanak Dev)
Book II (Guru Hargobind to Guru Tegh Bahadur)
Book III (Guru Angad to Guru Arjun Dev)
Book IV (Guru Gobind Singh)
Book V (Sikh Martyrs)
Book VI (Banda Singh Bahadur & Rise of the Sikhs)
Book VII (Maharaja Ranjit Singh & thereafter)

FOREWORD

Moral and religious instruction, I am glad to find, is now being rehabiliated in our schools. Our country is secular, it is true, but there is no denying the fact that religious and moral education has a very useful function to serve.

Modern psychology has emphasized that, if the child is given proper guidance at his formative stages, it will greatly help integrate his personality. The example of the teacher and his relations with students have a deep impression on the minds of students. Moral instruction, I feel, is better given by example than by precept.

The great figures of the past, specially the heroes of history, have shown mankind how to fight successfully against evil and face the challenges, from time to time.

This book tells the story of the struggle of the Sikhs against the tyrannical and oppressive rule of the Muslim Kings of India. The struggle was no longer simply for self-preservation. It aimed at wresting power from the fanatic foreign Mughals and Pathans and establishing Sikh Rule in the Panjab. After the death of Guru Gobind Singh at Nanded in 1708, Baba Banda Singh became the secular leader of the Sikhs. Under him the Sikhs conquered a great part of the Panjab but they had to suffer great reverses. Many, including Baba Banda Singh, were taken prisoners and paraded through the streets of Delhi. Thousands of Sikhs were martyred, but the Khalsa did not accept defeat. They continued their struggle until, in 1768, they finally occupied Lahore, and became the masters of the territory between the Indus and the Jhelum.

I sincerely hope that this series of sikh history books will go a long way in moulding the lives of the young Indian students.— Kartar Singh

CONTENTS

1. A Bairagi becomes a Saint-Soldier 7
2. Divine Help and Popular Supprt 12
3. Lessons in Self-Help 15
4. His Army 19
5. Banda Punishes Evil-Doers 24
6. Sarhind 29
7. Ghurani and Malerkotla 34
8. At His Capital 38
9. His Achievements 42
10. Last Stand at Gurdas Nangal 46
11. Set-back and Recovery 50
12. Traitors Punished 53
13. Vengeance 57
14. Policy of Conciliation 61
15. Khalsa Army Organised 66
16. Persecutions and Relaxation Again 69
17. Khalsa Declared a State 73
18. Ram Rauni Besieged 77
19. A Significant Contrast 82
20. Liberators 89
21. The Durrani Defeated 97
22. Fresh Conquests and More Sufferings 103
23. Final Occupation of Lahore 109

Baba Banda Singh Bahadur

1

A BAIRAGI BECOMES A SAINT-SOLDIER

In the previous book, you read the story of Baba Banda Singh Bahadur, the great Sikh martyr. Here you will read the story of what he did as a great Sikh hero, as a builder of the Sikh power. You will read how he won victories over the tyrannical, fanatic Mughal rulers, how he worked for the good of the people, and how he became the founder of the Sikh rule in the Punjab.

As you know, he was born on October 27, 1670, to a Rajput ploughman in Kashmir. He was thus about four years younger than Guru Gobind Singh; for the latter was born on December 26, 1666. He was named Làchhman Dev. While yet in his teens, he lost interest in the worldly, household life. He became a *Bairagi*. He took the name of Madho Das. He wandered from place to place. He came to Nasik on the banks of the Godavari in the Deccan. There he became a disciple of a Yogi named Aughar Nath. After the latter's death, he moved on along the river bank, till he came to Nander. There he built a small cottage for himself outside the city. He became famous for his magical and *tantric* powers. He took delight in practising tricks of magic on his visitors.

In the last week of September, 1708, Guru Gobind Singh came to Nander. He learnt of Bairagi Madho Das. He visited his cottage. The Bairagi tried his magic powers on the Guru.

But no magic could prevail against the latter. He gave up. He was conquered. He fell at the Guru's feet. Saying, 'I am your *banda*, your slave. Accept me as such. Let me be named Banda.' He was baptized and he was given the name of Banda Singh. Throughout his life, he was known by the title of Banda Singh, a title which he chose for himself. Soon, the Guru conferred on him the title of 'Bahadur'. Thus he came to be called Banda Singh Bahadur. But he was more popularly known as Banda Bahadur. In an instant he was a changed man. He was no longer a *Bairagi*. He had now become a fully fledged Sikh, a disciple of Guru Gobind Singh, a saint-soldier, a member of the Khalsa brotherhood. By adopting the title of 'Singh', he ceased to be a meek, inactive, peace-loving sadhu. He was transformed into Guru Gobind Singh's lion, a hero, a saint-soldier, ready to fight the tyrants, to conquer or die in the name of his Master.

He soon acquainted himself with the early history of the Sikhs and Sikhism, with the lofty ideals of Guru Nanak—Gobind Singh, and with the efforts made by them towards raising a nation of saint-warriors. He learnt about the martyrdom of Guru Arjan Dev and Guru Tegh Bahadur. He learnt about the cold-blooded murder of the Guru's younger sons at Sarhind; about the hardships and sufferings borne, and the sacrifices made by the Guru; of the wholesale persecution of millions of non-Muslims by the Mughals.

Then, it happened at that time that Guru Gobind Singh was stabbed by a Pathan, who had been sent for that purpose by the governor of Sarhind. This act of treachery filled Banda Singh with fury. His blood boiled within him. His martial spirit was up and active. He begged the Guru to allow him to proceed to the Punjab in order to punish the cruel, crafty, fanatic tyrants and their agents there.

Guru Gobind Singh had become disabled on account of the assassin's blow. As a matter of fact, he died on that account a few days later. But for that physical disability, he would himself have returned to the Punjab to continue his struggle against the Mughal tyrants. Under the circumstances, he had no other course left open to him but to accede to Banda Singh's request. He decided, therefore, to entrust the military command of the Khalsa to his charge. He chose him as his political and military successor. He made him the Commander of the Khalsa. He entrusted him with the noble and arduous task of continuing the war against the cruel, fanatic Mughal tyrants. The task assigned to him was that of liberating the country from the tyrannical Mughal rule.

Guru Gobind Singh's wars had all been defensive. He had never led any offensive expedition against Aurangzeb or any of his local deputies. In all his wars, whether against the Hindu hill-chiefs or against the Mughal officers, he had always been on the defensive. He had fought when attacked. He had taken to the sword as a last resort, in self-defence, and for self-preservation. He had won victories. But he had never occupied any territory, taken any prisoners, or taken possession of the defeated enemies' wealth. But Banda Singh was to go a step further. He was to take the offensive. He was to attack, fight, and conquer. He was to fight battles, not merely in order to cripple the Mughal power, but to destroy it, root and branch, to uproot and finish it off altogether. His wars were to be wars of conquest, and not merely wars of selfdefence. He was to acquire independent power for the Khalsa. He was to found a political Khalsa Raj in the Punjab.

Accordingly, Guru Gobind Singh readily acceded to Banda Singh's request. He appointed him Commander of the Khalsa. He bade him get ready to leave for the Punjab. On the eve of his departure, the Guru called him to his side. As we know, on account of the murderer's attack, the Guru was then confined to bed. He wanted to give Banda Singh his parting advice and to confer on him some gifts. He gave him the title of 'Bahadur', saying, 'In all that you do, you will always act as a brave saint-warrior.' He then gave him five arrows from his own quiver as a pledge of victory, saying, 'If you ever find yourself in a hopeless situation, think of the Guru and God, and shoot one of these arrows. You will get divine help and guidance.' He bestowed on him a flag and a drum, saying, 'They will serve as emblems of temporal authority.'

For his guidance, he gave him the following five commandments :

(1) Remain pure; never touch another's wife.
(2) Always think the truth, speak the truth, and act the truth; or, be true in thought, word, and deed;
(3) Regard yourself as a servant of the Khalsa, which is to be regarded as the Guru in future;
(4) Do not found a sect of your own; and
(5) Do not let victories elate you or kingly pride turn your head.

Furthermore, a council of five *Piaras* or beloved ones was appointed to assist him. It consisted of Bhais Binod Singh, Kahan Singh, Baj Singh, Daya Singh and Ran Singh. Twenty more select Sikhs were told to accompany him. The Guru also gave him *Hukmnamas* or letters addressed to Sikhs all over the country. In them the Sikhs were called upon to acknowledge Banda Singh as their leader, and to fight under his banner.

Thus raised to the position of Jathedar or Leader of the Khalsa, Commander of the Khalsa forces, Banda Singh left for the Punjab. He was to continue the struggle with the

10

Mughal rulers, and to put an end to their tyranny and oppression. He was to endeavour to liberate the country from the foreign Mughal rule. He was to replace those foreign rulers by such sons of the soil as, inspired by patriotism, would act equitably in the interests of the people as a whole.

Surely, it was a gigantic task. The Mughal empire, at that time, was the biggest and most powerful in the world. It possessed unlimited resources in men, money, and war-material. Baba Banda Singh, on the other hand, had no regularly trained army. He had to raise it from amongst the Sikhs, who had been, for long, subjected to the severest persecution by the Mughals. He did not possess the means and resources to acquire the essential necessities of war. He had to equip his soldiers as well as he could. He had to provide them rations, weapons, and other war-materials.

All this was no easy task. But Banda Singh was sure that, with his Master's blessings, he would achieve success. So he set forth with a firm resolve to accomplish the great and difficult task assigned to him. He was determined to do his best, 'heart within and God overhead'.

2

DIVINE HELP AND POPULAR SUPPORT

Accompanied by his twenty-five Sikh companions, Banda Singh hastened towards his destination. Soon, however, he was face to face with financial difficulties. From where to get the much and daily needed money ? He had full faith in God. 'I am a soldier of God Almighty,' he said to himself. 'My mission is holy. My aim is to punish those who have forgotten Him, who are mercilessly oppressing His children. Surely He will help me; He will not let me fail for want of funds; He will supply my needs. I shall pray to Him. He will answer my prayer.'

His companions had the same faith and conviction. They said, 'Let us pray together.' So they offered an *ardas* or congregational prayer. They invited the aid of the Almighty. Having done that, they continued their march. They were sure, all the time, that He would soon end their financial difficulties. And He did so. When they were in the neighbourhood of Bharatpur, they came across a trader, as if by chance. In reality, God had sent him that way in response to their prayer. He carried a large sum of money. It was his *Daswandh*, meant for the Guru's treasury. Every Sikh is enjoined upon to set apart one-tenth of his income for charitable and religious purposes. This is called *Daswandh*. In the Gurus' time, this rule was strictly observed. The amount was regularly remitted to the Gurus' treasury, either direct or through a *Masand*. He learnt of Banda Singh's mission. He learnt that Guru Gobind Singh had appointed him his deputy and Jathedar of the Khalsa.

12

Thereupon, he offered the money to Banda Singh. This was timely help, indeed. God had answered their prayer. Banda Singh was enabled to continue his march without any further worries.

As he proceeded further, he attracted popular interest and attention. People learnt that he was a deputy of Guru Gobind Singh. They believed that he could grant their wishes just as his Master, Guru Gobind Singh, could. They flocked to him to pay their homage and to get his blessings. He did not sent away any one disappointed. He blessed them all. He prayed for them all. He prayed for the success and prosperity of all who visited him. His visitors were not Hindus alone, but Muslims as well. He enjoined them all to remember and think of God, and to repeat the Sacred Name of *Waheguru.* In this way, he won the hearts of all who met him. As he went along, he became more and more popular with and respected by all sections of the people, including a large number of Muslims.

Besides his saintly blessings, his charity and princely generosity won the people's hearts. His charity and generosity knew no bounds. He was ever ready to help the needy with plenteous gifts. He paid all in gold *mohars.* None would receive less than a gold *mohar,* no matter how minor or insignificant the service rendered by him. An oilman supplying oil for his torches, a potter offering a few cups and pitchers, a sweeper bringing in some fuel—every one of them received a gold *mohar.* All this added to his popularity. It endeared him to the people's hearts.

As he went along, people learnt of his mission. They learnt that he had been deputed by Guru Gobind Singh to fight and finish off the fanatic foreign Mughal rule. Men endowed with brave hearts and martial spirits joined him as soldiers. Others contributed money and material to enable him to meet his daily increasing requirements. Thus he was enabled to gradually acquire men, money, and war-material needed for his campaign.

14

3

LESSONS IN SELF-HELP

Baba Banda Singh and his companions continued their march to Punjab. He found the people plunged in misery. Constant oppression had dulled their spirits. Most of them had become docile, servile, meek, and humble, like dumb-driven cattle. They had lost dignity, self-respect and manliness. They bore all oppression with abject meekness. They were cowardly and lacked self-reliance. They never thought of opposing their oppressors, or protesting against the excesses committed against them.

Banda Singh felt sorry for them. He wanted to inspire them with manly courage and self-reliance. He wanted to teach them to help themselves. Soon, an opportunity came to him to put his ideas into practice. As he reached the Bangar territory, near Hissar, he found that the tract was notorious for occasional raids of professional dacoits. One day he learnt that a group of dacoits was marching upon the village where he was stationed. He also learnt that the residents of the village were preparing to leave their hearths and homes to seek shelter in the neighbouring jungle. He felt sorry for them. He tried to check them. He exhorted them to stand against the raiders. He met the village Panches for the purpose. But they were too cowardly to entertain any such idea. They pleaded, 'We cannot stand against them. They are coming to take away our wealth. If we oppose them, they will take our lives as well, and take away also our women and girls. All happens as God wills. We are used to such raids. Leave us to our fate, and save yourself.'

15

Banda Singh was furious against this line of thought. He said, 'You are cowards, mean, and miserable cowards, all of you. Don't blame God. He will certainly help you, if you help yourselves. He does not side with doers of wrong and evil. Take courage, good men ! Imbibe the spirit of self-help and self-reliance. Be prepared for self-defence. I shall help you. Meet and defeat the raiders.'

But the Panches woefully shook their heads. They refused to make any response to his appeal. They argued that their safety lay in running away before the raiders arrived.

Banda Singh thought, 'If the Panches run away, the population will follow suit. I must prevent this.' So thinking, he locked up the Panches in a house. With a small band of Sikhs, he marched out to oppose the robbers. His attack was unexpected, sudden, bold, and severe. The robbers could not withstand it. They took to their heels. They ran away, leaving all the booty of their previous plunders. Their leader, however, was captured. All who came to rescue him, were killed or driven away. Now the villagers were emboldened. They got ready to strike a blow in their own defence. Banda Singh released the Panches. He ordered them to pursue the robbers. They did so. They and their fellow-villagers chased the robbers to their very homes in a neighbouring village.

This act of daring bravery was the beginning of the glorious career of this hero. It won him great fame and popularity. Quite often, thereafter, he was called upon to protect villages from plundering parties. He always, and most readily, responded to such appeals for help. He now publicly proclaimed that he would protect the poor and the helpless against all robbers, as well as against all official tyrants. He added, 'I want the people to live in safety, peace, and harmony. I shall ever help them to achieve this. For such service, I expect or desire no reward or return from the people, except simple necessities of life. And these, too, only from those who can give freely of their own accord.' He also invited people to enter the fold of the Khalsa Brotherhood. 'All who do so,' he added, 'will get a share in the lands that we shall conquer.'

Needless to say, that the appeal met with ample response.

It should be remembered that the dacoits made no communal distinction between their victims. They plundered Muslims, as well as non-Muslims. The official tyrants also made no communal distinction between the victims of their tyranny. They tyrannized over all, at their own will and pleasure. They were actually in league with the dacoits. They had, as their share, a fixed percentage out of the total proceeds of the dacoits' successful raids. Like wise Banda Singh also, made no communal distinction between those he would help and protect. Hence, he grew popular with all sections of the people. They, Muslims as well as non-Muslims, began to look upon him as their champion and protector against dacoits and official tyrants. He fully justified their confidence in him.

Once, later on, people from the neighbourhood of Sadhaura came to Banda Singh. They complained to him of the cruel and high-handed treatment which they suffered from their landlords. They begged him to rescue them from their landlords' tyranny. Banda Singh heard them with interest and patience. He made no direct reply. He ordered one of his men to open fire on them. They were, naturally, astonished at this strange reply to their representation. They asked him what it meant, why had he given such orders? He said, 'You deserve no other reply or treatment. You are thousands in number. The landlords are only a few. You are so weak and cowardly that a mere handful of them can hold down and keep in fear thousands of you. You feel helpless against them. Such cowards have no right to live. Why cannot you help yourselves ? Why should not the Khalsa of Guru Gobind Singh feel strong enough to redress their own wrongs ? Why should they go about begging for help, instead of helping themselves ? Do you now understand why I gave that order ?'

They understood what he meant. They went back. They turned out the landlords and took possession of their lands. Their example was followed in other parts of the country. The result was that the tillers of the soil became its masters. In the course of time, the curse of the *Zamindari* system was lifted from the Punjab. In many parts of Northern India this system remained intact for over two hundred years more.

4

HIS ARMY

Banda Singh and his companions continued their march towards their destination. In due course, they reached the villages of Sehri and Khanda, in the pargana of Kharkhanda. From there, he despatched the *Hukmnamas* of Guru Gobind Singh to the leading Sikhs of the Punjab, calling upon them to join him in the noble and praiseworthy task of uprooting the tyrannical, fanatic, and foreign rule of the Mughals. His companions also wrote a large number of letters to the leading Sikhs all over the country. In these letters they wrote that Banda Singh had been appointed Jathedar of the Khalsa by the Guru himself. It was, therefore, the duty of every Sikh to join and follow him. They added that Banda Singh was coming to punish Wazir Khan, governor of Sarhind, and his Hindu assistant, Sucha Nand, for having butchered the Guru's two younger sons. He would also punish the hill-rajas who had ill-treated the Guru and his people.

This produced a miraculous effect on the minds of the Sikhs. They were already burning with rage against Wazir Khan and others for their cruelties. Thousands of them flocked to Banda Singh from all quarters, ready to fight and die under his banner. In a few months, the whole Sikhs peasantry was up in arms to wreack vengeance on Wazir Khan and others.

There were three classes of men who joined Banda Singh in his campaign.

19

The first class was comprised of true and loyal Sikhs. They were those who had sat at the feet of Guru Gobind Singh. They had thus imbibed the heroic fire and spirit round the Guru's military successor in a spirit of devotion and self-sacrifice. They were eager to carry on the crusade against the enemies of their country and religion. Booty, or any kind of personal ambition or self-interest, was not their motive. On the contrary, hundreds sold their belongings, purchased arms, and flocked to the new leader. They were all firmly determined either to win the fight against the century-old enemies of their faith and people, or to achieve martyrdom. They were crusaders, eager to win the crown of victory or to drink the cup of martyrdom. Even when the tide turned against him, these selfless, devoted soldiers of God, Guru Gobind Singh's saint-warriors, remained with him to the last. Thousands of them bore untold hardships with him, and never thought of saving themselves. Thousands of them died of fatigue and starvation during the sieges of Banda Singh's fortresses. Thousands of them were captured, tortured, and executed by the Mughal government. But not a single of them gave up his faith or deserted Banda Singh in order to save his life. They all fell as heroic martyrs in the great and noble campaign for their country's liberation.

The second class consisted of paid soldiers. They had been recruited and sent on to Banda Singh by such chieftains as Ram Singh and Tilok Singh of the Phul family. These chieftains could not venture to join the army of Banda Singh in person. But they fully sympathized with his praiseworthy enterprise. They desired to render all possible help for its success. Later on, Banda Singh himself recruited paid soldiers under his banner. Such soldiers included a large number of Muhammedans also. The latter enjoyed full religious liberty, including that of saying Namaz and Azan.

The third class was entirely composed of irregulars. They were people who were attracted to Banda Singh by prospects of plunder and revenge. Most of them were professional dacoits and robbers. They were men of reckless daring. They hailed the movement; for it provided a golden opportunity to them. It offered them prospects of plundering cities and towns, instead of solitary wayfarers or caravans of merchants. Among the irregulars there were number of peasants and others who rushed in, at the time of attack on a town or city, to wreak their vengeance upon their personal enemies and oppressors.

It was this class of people who were mostly responsible for indiscriminate murder, destruction, and loot during Banda Singh's expeditions. They were under no discipline. They had no one at their head, no leader, whose orders they could be expected to obey. There was none who could regulate their actions and movements. They did not conduct themselves in the manner desired by Banda Singh. When attacking any town or city, Banda Singh, invariably, told his soldiers not to harm those people who offered no opposition, those who were not, or had not been, in league with tyrants, and who had done no wrong. Such people were to be spared from plunder and murder. The soldiers were to spare the lives of the Hindus, who showed their *choti*, the tuft of hair on their heads, and of those Muhammedans who offered an unconditional surrender. But the irregulars did not heed these instructions. Their sole aim was plunder or private vengeance. When a city fell, they rushed in and began to kill and loot all whom they could find, and to burn and destroy their houses.

Here, for example, is what they did when Samana was conquered. This town was the residence of Sayyed Jalal-ud-Din, the executioner of Guru Tegh Bahadur. Sashal Beg and

21

Bashal Beg, the executioners of the two younger sons of Guru Gobind Singh at Sarhind, had also been residents of Samana. So the town was strongly hated by the Sikhs. Samana was one of the richest towns in the locality. It was mostly inhabited by high-placed Sayyads and Mughals. When it fell, the Sikh soldiers were busy sacking the houses of the three executioners and searching for the treasure of the Faujdar and the Mughal Amirs. The plunderers or irregulars, on the other hand, were busy in their own trade. They looted people and burnt their houses most brutally and indiscriminately. They spared none.

Peasants from the neighbouring villages also rushed in to wreak vengeance upon their personal enemies. They massacred the latter and their families. They looted and set fire to their houses. The irregulars avenged their personal animosities in a most reckless manner. They paid their persecutors in their own coin and, perhaps, with heavy compound interest.

During the last hundred years, the Sikhs, had been subjected to innumerable persecutions and indignities at the hands of Muhammedan rulers and officials. The Sikhs therefore, were naturally enraged against the rulers. They vied with one another in massacring them, some with a view of avenging their own wrongs, others with the object of punishing the tyrants. Thus, before nightfall, the beautiful town of Samana, with its palatial buildings, was converted into a heap of ruins, never to regain its past glory. Ten thousand lives are said to have been lost, the majority among them being Mughals. Those who remained, left this place for ever.

Banda Singh did not like such loot, destruction, and massacre. But he was helpless under the circumstances.

22

The irregulars were, at the same time, most dangerous and unreliable allies. Often, they deserted Banda Singh in the thick of battle when they feared a defeat. Sometimes they took to their heels at the very sight of the enemy's guns and cannons. Many times, even the paid soldiers would follow their example and desert the crusaders. But at the time of victory, they rushed back to plunder the conquered city.

5

BANDA PUNISHES EVIL-DOERS

Guru Gobind Singh had declared, again and again, that he had been sent by God to punish and destroy cruel, wicked evil-doers and tyrants. After doing as much as God willed and permitted him to do, he appointed Banda Singh his military successor. He deputed him to carry on the struggle against the Mughal tyrants and other evil-doers. His mission was to liberate the country from the tyrannical Mughal rule. That rule was still foreign in most of its essentials. It was as severe and unsympathetic as it had been in the days of Guru Nanak. He had then declared it as a rule of 'tigers and hounds'. Like his Master, Banda Singh believed that he had been assigned by God the duty of punishing and destroying the cruel, wicked evil-doers and tyrants. These cruel, wicked evil-doers and tyrants of the time were mostly Mughal officials and their agents. They were all Muhammedans. Hence, Banda Singh believed himself to be, and was regarded by the people, as the scourge of those Muhammedans, an instrument of divine wrath against them. He was to punish them for their crimes and beastly sins. Hence, he began to be looked upon as the champion of the down-trodden, the defender of the faith.

As he marched along, oppressed Hindus of various places resorted to him for help and protection. They complained to him against their Mughal officials and Muhammedan neighbours and effective response to every such complaint.

It will be impossible to tell here about all the complaints which Banda Singh received and redressed. A few instances are given here.

Once he received a series of complaints against the Mughal ruler of Kapuri, a town about six kilometers from Sadhaura. His name was Qadam-ud-Din. He was a veritable beast. He treated the people with the utmost cruelty. He was a tyrant and a vicious man of the worst type. He was notorious for his lustful campaigns. Stories of his campaigns are still current in Kapuri and its neighbourhood, even after more than two centuries and a half. There was hardly a family in the town whose honour had not been destroyed by his lust. There was hardly a handsome woman, Hindu or Muslim, in or near the town, whose chastity had not been attacked by him. His men rode about in the territory in search of *shikar* for him. They waylaid Hindu marriage-parties, snatched away the new brides, and made them over to their beastly, lustful master. He was thus a terror to all, Muslims, and non-Muslims of the *ilaqa*.

This was more than a Sikh like Banda Singh could tolerate or ignore. He was receiving complaint after complaint against Qadam-ud-Din from the people on all sides. He decided to attend to no other business till he had properly punished the cruel, depraved ruler of Kapuri. He fell upon the town early one morning. Qadam-ud-Din could not stand against the Sikhs for long. He was slain. The strong-holds of his debaucheries were set on fire. His ill-gotten wealth was scattered to the four winds.

Soon afterwards, Banda Singh had to turn his attention to Sadhaura. It was another place of oppression. Its ruler, Usman Khan, was the same man who had tortured to death the great Muslim saint, Sayyad Budhu Shah. Why ? Simply because he had helped Guru Gobind Singh in the battle of

25

Bhangani. The Hindus of this place complained to Banda Singh saying, 'The Muhammedans are subjecting us to all sorts of indignities and cruelties. They dishonour our women-folk. They do not allow us to perform our religious rites and ceremonies. They do not permit us to cremate our dead. They slaughter cows in our lands and streets, before our doors and houses. Then they leave their blood and intestines there. There is none to check them. We have learnt with joy that you and your companions come as defenders of the faith, as champions of the oppressed and the weak. We have come to you for help. Save us, we beseech you, Saint-Soldier of the Guru.'

Banda Singh was much enraged on hearing all this. He at once marched upon Sadhaura. The news of this attack spread like wild fire. The peasantry and other people of the neighbourhood had been subjected to untold cruelties and oppressions. They had been silently and helplessly bearing all this for years. Now they got a favourable chance for rising against the oppressors and wreaking vengeance on them. They joined the invaders and rushed into the town. The Sikhs directed their attention to Usman Khan and other oppressors. But the mob got out of hand. Even Banda Singh found it impossible to control it or to hold its fury in check. The frightened Sayyads and Sheikhs had taken shelter in the *haveli* of Sayyad Budhu Shah. They thought that the martyred Sayyad had been a friend of Guru Gobind Singh; so the Guru's Sikhs would respect the martyr's mansion. They would not attack it.

But the Sikhs were powerless. They were comparatively small in number. The mob out-numbered them many times. They were unacquainted with the place. The infuriated peasantry were inspired or fired with a spirit of revenge against their persecutors. They worked havoc here as

26

elsewhere. They had borne, silently and helplessly, the oppression of those people. Now they had got their chance. Nothing short of wholesale massacre could satisfy them. All the inmates of the *haveli* were put to the sword. On that account, since then, the place has been called the *Qatalgarhi* or Slaughter-house.

On another occasion, the Hindus of Chhat, near Banur, appealed to Banda Singh against the tyranny and high-handedness of the local Muhammedans. They made their complaints in the most pleading language. They added, 'The loose morality and religious intolerance of these tyrants are a terror to our faith and honour. Help us, O champion of the down trodden, defender of the faith!'

As usual, Banda Singh acted at once. He fell upon Chhat, punished the evil-doers, occupied the town, and placed it under a Sikh official.

With the rising of the Sikhs, many Hindus and Muhammedans had taken *Amrit* and become Sikhs. Many of these converts belonged to the village of Unarsa, in the pargana of Deoband. Jalal Khan, the ruler of that area, ordered all these new Sikhs to be imprisoned and persecuted. One of them informed Banda Singh of their pitiable condition and appealed to him for help. The Hindus of Deoband also complained to him that Jalal Khan was treating them most cruelly. They appealed for help and deliverance.

On hearing these complaints, Banda Singh crossed the Jamna at Rajghat. He marched upon Saharanpur, on his way to Jalal Khan's city of Jalalabad. Saharanpur was one of the principal strongholds of bigoted Muhammedans. The ruler of the place, Ali Hamid Khan, was terror-struck on hearing of the Sikhs' advance. That very night he deserted Saharanpur and fled to Delhi, with all his family and property. The town-people and officers offered stout resistance to Banda Singh but it was not very long or effective. The Sikhs were more than a match for them. They gained possession of the town. The offending Muhammedans were subjected to indiscriminate plunder and slaughter.

From here Banda Singh directed his attention to Behat, a small town north of Saharanpur. Complaints had reached him that the *Peerzadas* of that place were notorious religious fanatics, that they ill-treated the Hindus, and that they took particular pleasure in slaughtering cows in the streets of the town. At the request of the aggrieved people of the place, a party was despatched by Banda Singh to Behat. The town was attacked and sacked. The *Peerzadas* were put to the sword.

Then Banda Singh proceeded towards Jalalabad. He reduced every town and village that fell on the way. Jalalabad was besieged. But it was not an easy job to reduce it. Heavy rains had set in. The surrounding country was flooded with rain-water. The flooded river Krishna practically washed the town and the fort walls. The siege had to be lifted after twenty days and nights of incessant heroic efforts.

Banda Singh and his Sikhs were now looked up to by the non-Muslim population as defenders of the faith, champions of the oppressed. Complaints poured in from all places. There was hardly a village, town, or city where the non-Muslim population was not subjected to cruelty and oppression by the Muhammedan officials and the local Muhammedans. The oppressed people began to take their complaints to Banda Singh. Every such complaint excited his fury against the tyrants. Banda Singh and his Sikhs considered it their religious duty to help their suffering brethren. They discharged this duty without caring for their own comfort or safety. No wonder that they won the people's respect and admiration.

6

SARHIND

As Banda Singh marched on, he attacked and conquered all strongholds of Muslim oppression, like Samana, Kapuri, Sadhaura, and Chhat. In every place he punished the Muhammedan officers and others for their tyranny and oppression. Then he advanced on Sarhind.

It was at Sarhind that the two younger sons of Guru Gobind Singh, Baba Zorawar Singh and Baba Fateh Singh had been brutally tortured to death. This cruel, bloody deed had been done at the orders of Nawab Wazir Khan. None of the people there had raised even the faintest voice against these inhuman murders. The Guru had, therefore, condemned and crushed the city, its cruel officers, and its heartless people. Because of all this, the place was regarded by the Guru's followers as most hateful and mean. They burnt with a longing for an apportunity to wreak their vengeance upon the hated, murderous town, its governor, and his agents like Sucha Nand. It was, indeed, looked upon as a sacred duty to take part in the attack upon Sarhind. The desire for martyrdom in this crusade had brought thousands of Sikhs from all parts of the Punjab. The number of plunderers who followed the Sikhs for booty's sake was also steadily increasing. Preparations for an attack on Sarhind were made. This filled a new spirit in the Sikhs. The heavens resounded with their loud and joyous war-cries.

At this stage, a Hindu officer of Sarhind appeared in the Sikh camp. He was a nephew of Sucha Nand. He had one thousand men with him. He said to Banda Singh, 'I have left the Nawab's service on account of his high-handedness towards me and my family. I have come with my devoted followers to join the Khalsa. I want to wreak vengeance.' In reality, he had come to play the part of a traitor. He had been deputed by Wazir Khan and Sucha Nand to play a trick upon Banda Singh. He was told to do away with Banda Singh as soon as he could find an opportunity to do so. 'If you fail in your design,' he was further told, 'you should so act during the battle as to lead to an utter defeat of the Sikhs.' Banda Singh believed his story and allowed him to join the camp.

Naturally enough, Wazir Khan was filled with fear of vengeance for his excesses against Guru Gobind Singh and the cold-blooded murder of his infant sons. He proclaimed *Jehad* or a religious war against the *Kafirs* or 'infidel' Sikhs. The Muhammedans were exhorted to kill every Sikh that they came across. Thousands of Muhammedans, from far and near, gathered at Sarhind. Wazir Khan also combined with him four or five noted Faujdars and Zamindars. Sher Muhammad Khan, ruler of Maler Kotla, was one of them. Thus he had a large army at his back.

Banda Singh instructed his commanders to direct their attention to wazir Khan and his supporters. He told them to spare the lives of the Hindus who showed their *choti* or the tuft of hair on their heads. They were also to spare the lives of all those Muhammedans who offered an unconditional surrender. They were strictly forbidden to touch the enemy's women-folk. He said to them, 'We are going to punish these people but not because they are Muhammedans. We are to punish them because of their being political persecutors of innocent people. We are to punish them for their cruelty and religious intolerance towards their poor, helpless subjects and neighbours. We shall punish even such Hindus as are guilty of these offences. Therefore, there should be no indiscriminate massacre of the Muhammedans anywhere. No one should attack the honour of women of the conquered enemy.'

Wazir Khan learnt of Banda Singh's projected attack on Sarhind. He marched out in person with a large army of about twenty-five thousand men. In his army, he had cavalry, musketeers, archers and artillery. He had also a long line of elephants. On the other hand, Banda Singh did not have a sufficient supply of horses for his men. Long spears, arrows, and swords were the only weapons-of-war with the Sikhs. They had no guns or cannon. They had received no regular training as soldiers. But they had something which their enemies totally lacked. They had zest and determination born of religious fervour, patriotism, and zeal for sacrifice. They were fighting for their faith and country. They were determined to win victory over the enemies of their faith and country, or to become martyrs.

As soon as the battle began, and the Mughal army opened fire, the robbers and dacoits took to their heels. They wanted to gain booty, not to lose their lives. The next to flee were the one thousand men of the wile, treacherous nephew of Sucha Nand. Some mercenaries or paid soldiers also deserted. Only the faithful Sikhs were left to fight out the battle. They were fired with the resolve to win or die with their faces towards the enemies of their faith and country.

The fight was long, bloody, and severe. Banda Singh rushed to the forefront of his army and boldly led his men to the attack. The Sikhs were very much encouraged by this bold movement of their leader. With loud shouts of 'Sat Sri Akal' and 'Waheguruji ki Fateh' they fell upon the Muhammedans. The Muhemmedan force was unable to

31

stand the fierce, repeated attacks of the Khalsa. Religious fervour and political zeal at last triumphed over the cannon and the larger number of Mughals. Wazir Khan himself was slain along with a large number of noted assistants. Sher Muhammad Khan, ruler of Maler Kotla, was among the slain.

Confusion arose in the Muhammedan ranks. The Khalsa rushed on them fiercely. 'Not a man of the army of Islam,' says a Muhammedan writer, 'escaped with more than his life and the clothes he stood in. Horsemen and footmen fell under the sword of the infidels (Sikhs), who pursued them as far as Sarhind.'

Wazir Khan's army was totally defeated and routed. Banda Singh and his Sikhs were now masters of the field. They ascribed this victory to *Waheguru*, the Almighty. Their loud and joyous shouts of '*Sat Sri Akal*' and '*Waheguruji ki Fateh*' rent the air. They marched upon the city of Sarhind, which was about sixteen kilometers from the field of battle.

The city was entered after some resistance. About five hundred Sikhs are said to have been lost in that scuffle. A Shahid Ganj now stands on the site where they were cremated.

The heartless Muhammedan population was subjected to indiscriminate plunder. The sentiments of the Sikh crusaders had been very much excited on account of the cold-blooded murder of the two infant sons of Guru Gobind Singh. Now, when they entered the accursed city after a bloody fight, the memory of that cruel deed inflamed the fire of their fury. Moreover, a host of plunderers rushed in from all sides. They were under no discipline. They could not be restrained. The city lost heavily in life and property. The

32

irregulars avenged their personal animosities in a most reckless manner. Banda Singh took care that no harm was done to any mosque or Muslim shrine. The mausoleum of Shaikh Ahmad Mujadid Ali Sani still stands there as it did before the conquest of Sarhind.

While Banda Singh was at Sarhind, a large number of Hindus and Muhammedans embraced Sikhism of their own free will. They were eager to win the Sikh hero's favours. A Muhammedan writer of those days says, 'The authority of the Sikhs extended to such an extent that many Hindus and Muhammedans had no alternative to obedience and submission. They adopted the Sikh faith and rituals. Their chief, Banda Singh, captivated the hearts of all towards his inclinations. When a Hindu or a Muslim came in contact with him, he addressed him by the title of Singh. Accordingly, Dindar Khan, a powerful ruler of the neighbourhood, was named Dindar Singh. Mir Nasir-ud-Din, the news-writer of Sarhind, became Mir Nasir Singh. In the same way, a large number of Muhammedans abandoned Islam and followed the path of Sikhism. They took solemn oaths and firm pledges to stand by him.'

Banda Singh now took in hand the administration of the territories he had conquered. Baj Singh, one of his companions and advisers from Nander, was appointed Subedar or Governor of Sarhind. Bhai Fateh Singh was confirmed in his appointment as Governor of Samana. Ram Singh, brother of Baj Singh, was appointed Governor of Thanesar jointly with Baba Binod Singh. Detachments were sent out to occupy the country to the south, the east and the west of Sarhind. The Mughal officials in all places submitted to Banda Singh. Soon, all the subordinate parganas fell into the Sikhs' hands.

7

GHURANI AND MALER KOTLA

Banda Singh had come to be looked upon as the defender of the faith and champion of the weak. It became a fashion with the people to approach him for redress of their grievances, big and small. And he invariably took prompt and effective action in every case.

One day, a Sikh *ragi* or musician, named Bulaqa Singh, complained to him against the Ram Raiyas of Ghurani, in the *thana* of Payal. Ram Raiyas are the followers of Ram Rai. He had been expelled from the Sikh brotherhood by his father, Guru Har Rai. He had been expelled because, in order to please Aurangzeb, he had changed the wording of a line of Guru Nanak's holy words or *Gurbani*. In that way he had acted against the injunctions and spirit of Sikhism. The Ram Raiyas have generally been inimical towards the Sikh Gurus and their disciples. In that village there lived a number of Khatris who were Masands of the establishment of Ram Rai. Bulaqa Singh said to Banda Singh, 'One day I happened to be at Ghurani. There is a Gurdwara of Guru Hargobind in that village. After the evening service of *Rahras* in that Gurdwara, I said *ardas* or prayer. When I repeated the words 'Khalsa Sahib, bolo ji Waheguru', (O Members of the Khalsa Brotherhood, utter Waheguru, the name of the Almighty God.) after the name of Guru Gobind Singh, the Ram Raiyas were enraged. They abused and assaulted me. They broke my harp. In their fit of fury, they used very abusive language towards Guru Gobind Singh.

34

An insult to his Master was more than Banda Singh could bear. Like a true and zealous disciple of the Guru that he was, he at once marched out of Sarhind to punish the slanderers. The Ram Raiya Masands were arrested, punished, and driven out of the village. A Sikh thana was established at Payal. Bulaqa Singh ragi was appointed Thanedar of the circle.

From here Banda Singh proceeded to Maler Kotla. He was not going there with the intention to plunder or destroy it. He was going there to perform what he thought was his religious duty. Now you may wonder why he did not intend to harm that city. Its ruler, Sher Muhammad Khan, had fought against him and the Sikhs. He had broken his oath on the Quran and fallen upon Guru Gobind Singh near the Sarsa stream. And what was the religious duty which he wanted to perform at Maler Kotla ? The answers to these questions are as follow :

It is true that Sher Muhammad Khan caused a good deal of trouble to Guru Gobind Singh. When the Mughal army attacked and besieged the Guru at Anandpur, Sher Muhammad Khan was among the attackers and besiegers. Of course, he had all his forces with him. After a prolonged siege, the besiegers sent a message to the Guru, saying, 'We urge you to vacate the fort and leave the city. We swear on the holy Quran that we shall do you no harm. You will not be attacked or molested. You may go wherever you like.' Guru Gobind Singh vacated the fort. As soon as the besiegers learnt of it, they fell upon him near Sarsa. Sher Muhammad Khan of Maler Kotla was among those who broke their solemn oath and attacked the Guru.

Some time afterwards, the Guru's two younger sons fell into the hands of Nawab Wazir Khan, Governor of Sarhind.

He ordered that they should be tortured to death. Sher Muhammad Khan was then present in the Nawab's court. He pleaded for the little innocent children. He advocated mercy to them, and endeavoured to obtain their release.

Guru Gobind Singh was later told to Sher Muhammad Khan's act of kindness and human sympathy. He felt grateful to him. His sense of gratitude made him forget and forgive the many troubles he had received at the Khan's hands. He blessed him. He offered fervent prayers for him.

Banda Singh knew that his Master had blessed and prayed for Sher Muhammad Khan of Maler Kotla. He, therefore, decided not to do any harm to the Khan's city. It may be added that the Sikhs have ever kept alive their sense of gratitude for Sher Muhammad Khan's act of kindness, tiny though it was. Like their Guru, they have forgotten and forgiven the evils and excesses committed by the Khan. They have never done any harm to his city, his descendants, and his people. Even during the storm of communal frenzy which swept the country in 1947, no harm, whatsoever, was done to Maler Kotla and its people who were mostly Muslims.

As regards the religious duty which Banda Singh wanted to perform at Maler Kotla, the Mughals' treacherous attack on Guru Gobind Singh near Sarsa, caused much confusion. Bibi Anup Kaur, a Sikh maidservant of the Guru's house, fell into Sher Muhammad Khan's hands. He carried her away to his city. He wanted to compel her to embrace Islam. He wanted to destroy her chastity. But the brave Sikh woman sacrificed her life at the altar of her faith and chastity. In order to save her honour, she thrust a dagger into her own heart and committed suicide. Sher Muhammad Khan, thereupon, quietly buried her in a grave. Now, Bibi

36

Anup Kaur had not embraced Islam. She had died a Sikh. Hence, she should have been cremated according to the Sikh rites. But she was buried as if she had been a Muhammedan.

Banda Singh was moved to hear this story. If Sher Muhammad Khan had not earned Guru Gobind Singh's blessings, Banda Singh would have wreaked vengeance on the Khan's city, as he had done on Nawab Wazir Khan's city of Sarhind. So, because of the Guru's blessings, the city was allowed to go unharmed.

Banda Singh said, however, that the brave Sikh woman's body should not be allowed to rot in a grave. He, therefore, marched on the town of Maler Kotla. There was no one there to offer any resistance. As you know, Sher Muhammad Khan had been killed in the battle of Sarhind. His sons, with all their families and belongings, had fled from the place. Banda Singh did not want to plunder or destroy Maler Kotla. So it was left unmolested and unharmed. Banda Singh directed his attention solely to the performance of the last rites of Bibi Anup Kaur. Her body was taken out of the grave and cremated according to the Sikh rites.

From here Banda Singh proceeded to Rai Kot. Its ruler offered no resistance. He acknowledged Banda Singh as his overlord.

8

AT HIS CAPITAL

In the course of a short time, Banda Singh had become master of the Punjab—east of Lahore, that is, from Panipat to Lahore. His power was thus well established over a fairly vast territory. His aim was to destroy the Mughal rule from the land altogether. He had destroyed it in this part of the Punjab. Its place had to be taken by someone. So he assumed royal authority. He fixed the fort of Mukhlispur as his capital. The fort had been occupied by him with the conquest of Sadhaura. It was a strong hill-fort, about half-way between the towns of Sadhaura and Nahan. It was in a most neglected condition when it was occupied by Banda Singh. He repaired it and gave it the name of Lohgarh or Iron Fort. It became the capital of the Sikh territories, with Banda Singh as the first Sikh ruler. Thus, he became the founder of Sikh rule.

The Sikh from all over the country now flocked to Banda Singh's standard in much larger numbers. They swelled the ranks of his volunteer-soldiers. Most of them were zealous, faithful Sikhs, dedicated to the cause of the holy war against the tyrannical, fanatical, foreign Mughal rule. Many of them had mortgaged their land and property, in order to equip themselves for the purpose. Others came in hopes of getting wealth and position under the rapidly rising power of Banda Singh and his companions.

Banda Singh was now a king in all but name. He was master of a vast territory. He governed it through his deputies. He commanded a large army of devoted followers. He had a capital and palaces to live in. He now struck coins like all kings. But unlike them, he did not strike the coins in his own name. He struck them in the name of his masters, Guru Nanak—Guru Gobind Singh. Like the Mughal coins, his coins had Persian inscriptions on both sides. The inscription on one side, translated into English, were as follows :

'By the grace of the True Lord is struck this coin in the two worlds :

The Sword of Nanak is the granter of all boons, and the victory is of Guru Gobind Singh, the King of Kings.'

The inscription on the other side was to the following effect :—

'Struck in the City of Peace, illustrating the beauty of civic life, and the ornament of the blessed throne.'

These were the titles and epithets used by him for his capital, just as the emperor's cities had their titles on their coins.

He also introduced an official seal for his *Hukmnamas* and *Farmans*, or order and letters patent. It bore an inscription in Persian which may be translated thus :—

'The Kettle and the Sword (symbols of Charity and Power), Victory, and ready Patronage, have been obtained from Guru Nanak—Gobind Singh.'

The inscription is expressive of his deep sense of devotion and loyalty to his Master.

Each Mughal Emperor used to introduce his own regal year. It started from the date of his coming to the throne. It was called *Sann -i-Jalus* or the year of accession. Like the Mughal Emperors, Banda Singh introduced his own Sammat or regal year. It commenced with the date of his conquest of Sarhind.

All this was obviously an imitation of the Mughal Emperors. It was intended to infuse in the Sikhs' minds a sense of equality with the ruling people. It was meant to impress them, to make them feel that they were in no way inferior to those who ruled over the land. If the Mughals had their capital, coins, seal, and the *Sann -i-Jalus*, they, too, had their own capital, coins, etc. But, as said already, their was a most striking difference between the two. The Mughal Emperors' coins and seals bore the Emperors' own names. But Banda Singh's coins and seal bore the names of Guru Nanak and Guru Gobind Singh. He claimed the Gurus as his guiding spirits and guardian angels. He proclaimed that it was from them that he had obtained his prosperity and power, Degh and Tegh.

As a result of his brilliant victories, Banda Singh established Sikh rule in a part of the Punjab. But he had no time to organize any regular system of administration. Still, during the very short time at his disposal, he had his best to improve the lot of the common man. He dedicated himself to the task of the ending the people's oppression and persecution at the hands of officials and others. He made no distinction between Sikhs, Hindus, and Muhammedans. He treated them all alike. Whenever he heard any complaint against any official or some other powerful person, he punished him without delay. He showed no mercy to such offenders. The rank, position, and creed of the offender never influenced his spirit of justice. He treated all criminal cases in a speedy, summary manner. This made him a terror of the tribe of petty officials. The people felt relieved and safe, for centuries past nobody had heard or cared for their sufferings and cries.

He used to tell his men, 'It is written in the Holy Granth that, "the best worship for a king is to be just". Those who do not administer justice are cast into hell. A king should practise justice. Thus spoke the Great Man (Guru Gobind Singh). If you call yourselves the Sikhs of the Great Man, do not practise sin and injustice. Raise up the Sikhs and smite those who do un-Sikh like acts. Bear the sayings of the Great Man in your hearts.'

Thus, Banda Singh's administration was manned by persons who avoided sin, and injustice, who bore the sayings of Guru Gobind Singh in their hearts. His was, therefore, a government of the people, for the people.

9

HIS ACHIEVEMENTS

It is indeed a pity that Banda Singh could not maintain the principality which he carved out at the beginning of his career. Still, even the short time for which he ran his administration, he carried out what, up to this day, is recognized as one of the best fiscal reforms. It has had a great influence on the subsequent history of the Punjab. He abolished the Zamindari System of the Mughals. In its place, he introduced peasant proprietorship.

The Zamindari System was for purposes of realizing land-revenue. A number of villages were entrusted to a prominent person. Usually he was a government official. He was made responsible for paying a fixed amount to the government as land-revenue for those villages. He was called a Zamindar or Land-Lord. He was free to collect from the cultivators whatever amounts he liked. In the course of time, the Zamindars became absolute proprietors of the land of the villages under them. They could employ or turn out cultivators at their sweet will. As long as they paid the fixed amount, the authorities did not interfere in their internal arrangements. They were more than autocratic kings in themselves. The cultivators were practically reduced to the position of slaves. The Zamindars oppressed them and made too large collections by force.

Now, the Sikhs were mostly from the agricultural classes. They knew where the shoe pinched. For a long time they had been groaning under the landlords' tyranny. So the first thing that the Sikhs did was to strike out this evil, root and branch. The Zamindari System was abolished. The tillers of the soil became its masters. A great and long-standing curse was thus lifted from the Punjab.

Banda Singh's victories produced another far-reaching beneficial result. He and his men had done much to help the oppressed people against the oppressors. The oppressors were mostly Muhammedans. The oppressed people were mostly non-Muslims. So the Sikhs succeeded in inspiring confidence in the minds of the non-Muslim people. The latter came to look upon the Sikhs as champions of the weak and defenders of the faith and country. Naturally, of course, the Sikhs were fired with a strong new zeal. They, too, began to look upon themselves as defenders of the faith and country. It became a fashion with the oppressed people to rush with their complaints to the Sikhs. Every such complaint excited the Sikhs against the officials and other oppressors. They considered it their religious duty to help their suffering brethern and to relieve their hardships. This could best be done by removing the Mughal officials. Accordingly, the Sikhs all over the country started on a career of conquest, and began to carry out their design. Inspired by religious zeal, they performed wonderful deeds of heroism. They carried everything before them. The haughty, fanatic Mughal officials were replaced by persons who could be trusted to be mild and just. In about two months, the Sikhs were able to reverse the centuries-old order of things. A new era of freedom from oppression was started under Sikh rule, which was just and sympathetic towards the people.

The very name of the Sikhs was a source of terror to evil-doers of all sorts. Even the sight of a Sikh horseman would be enough to unnerve a multitude of haughty, unbending officials and their followers. They became eagerly ready to mend themselves, in order to escape being singled out for punishment. On the other hand, every Sikh, of whatever status in life, felt that he had been raised by God above all his fellow-subjects. He felt that it was his destiny to be a ruler, a champion of the downtrodden and the weak, a friend of the needy and the foe of all tyrants.

According to an English writer, 'In all parts occupied by the Sikhs, all previous customs were strikingly and thoroughly reversed. Persons who used to be considered low and were despised, came to be regarded as worthy of respect. We know that scavengers and leather-dressers were regarded as the lowest among the low in India. But if a scavenger or leather-dresser left his home and joined Banda Singh, he would soon be raised to a high position. Very often he would, in a short time, return to his birth-place as its ruler, with the order of his appointment in his hand. As soon as he set foot within the boundaries of his village, the well-born and wealthy people went out to greet him. They escorted him home. When they arrived there, they stood before him with joined palms, awaiting his orders. Not a soul dared to question or disobey an order. Men who had often risked their lives in battlefields became so cowed down that they were afraid even to remonstrate.'

Banda Singh thus brought about a really remarkable revolution in the parts which he occupied and ruled.

Banda Singh's aim was nothing short of liberation of the country from the tyrannical, fanatical, foreign Mughal rule. He was the first among the Sikhs to think of founding a political raj. He fought battles, not merely to cripple Mughal power, but to destroy it, root and branch. But the task proved too great for him. The Mughal Emperor was too strong for him. The Emperor had at his disposal, the unlimited resources of the then greatest Empire in the world. Banda Singh lacked sufficient resources. He did not have the necessary men and material. Only the poor classes of the Sikhs joined him. His army consisted mostly of untrained peasants. Their number was altogether insufficient. The general masses of the Hindus kept themselves aloof. Nay, many of the Hindu chiefs took an active part against him. They were active supporters of the oppressive, fanatic Mughals. Because of all this, sadly Banda Singh's success was short-lived.

All the same, Banda Singh left a lasting mark on the character of the Sikhs. He fanned the fire of independence ignited by Guru Gobind Singh. He effected a revolution in the minds of the people. A will was created in the ordinary masses to resist tyranny, and to live and die for a common or national cause. The example set by Banda Singh and his companions was to serve as a beacon light for the people in the darker days to come. He was the first man to deal a severe blow to the cruel, fanatic Mughal rule in the Punjab. He broke the first sod in the conquest of that province by the Sikhs. He virtually succeeded in destroying the Muslim ruling class. Although it was forty years after his death that Lahore, the capital of the Punjab, was occupied by the Khalsa, and a regular Sikh rule was declared, yet it was Banda Singh Bahadur who laid the foundation of the Sikh Empire in 1710. He was the founder of Sikh rule.

10

LAST STAND AT GURDAS NANGAL

Banda Singh's success enraged the mighty Mughal Emperor. He issued strong, imperative orders to the Governor of Lahore. The latter was ordered to take immediate steps to kill or capture the Sikh Chief and his followers. He issued orders also to a number of Mughal and Hindu officials and chiefs. He ordered them to proceed with all their troops to help the armies of Lahore. On receipt of these orders, the Faujdars of Gujrat, Eminabad, Aurangabad, Pasrur, Batala, Patti, and Kalanaur, and the Hindu Rajas of Katauch and Jasrota, assembled their forces at Lahore, ready to proceed against Banda Singh.

Banda Singh was well aware of the preparations being made against him at Lahore. He decided to throw up a mud fortification at Kot-Mirza, a small village between Kalanaur and Batala. But before its defences could be completed, the combined Hindu and Muhammedan forces from Lahore fell upon the Sikhs. Banda Singh stood his ground so well that all were filled with amazement. In the first encounter he fought so heroically that 'he was very near effecting a complete defeat on the Imperial armies'. But he had no place where he could take stand. He was, therefore, obliged to fall back upon Gurdas Nangal.

Gurdas Nangal was the old village, now a heap of ruins, known as Bande-wali-Thehi. It was about six kilometres to the west of Gurdaspur. It had no regular fort. The Sikhs had to take shelter in the *ihata* or enclosure of Bhai Duni Chand.

This enclosure had a strong, massive wall around it. It was spacious enough to accommodate Banda Singh and his men. He made every effrot to strengthen his defences and to collect stores of rations and ammunition. A moat was dug round the enclosure and filled with water. He cut the Imperial Canal and small streams flowing from below the hills. Their water was allowed to spread. It made a quagmire round the place. It would serve to keep off the enemy.

Here the Sikhs made their stand. The besiegers kept 'so watchful a guard that not a blade of grass, not a grain of corn, could find its way in'. Occasionally, thousands of the besiegers attempted to storm the Sikh position. But all their attempts were defeated by a comparatively small handful of Sikhs. A muhammedan writer who was present, writes, 'The brave and the daring deeds of the Sikhs were wonderful. Twice or thrice a day, some forty or fifty of the Sikhs came out of their enclosure to gather grass for their cattle. When the combined Imperial forces, went to oppose them, they (Sikhs) made an end of the Mughals with arrows, muskets, and small swords. Then they disappeared. Such was the terror of the Sikhs and the Sikh Chief, that the commanders of the besieging armies prayed that God might so ordain things that Banda Singh would seek safety in retreat from the *garhi* or fortress.'

On several occasions, the Sikhs fell on the besiegers' camp, and carried away from there whatever they could lay their hands on. Baba Binod Singh would occasionally come out of the enclosure, and carry away eatables from the Bazar of the besiegers' camp. The whole camp was wonder-struck at the boldness of the old Sikh. All efforts to catch him proved futile.

The siege and struggle continued for several months.

There was great loss on both sides. The besiegers tightened their ring round the Sikhs' enclosure. Consequently, it became impossible for the Sikhs to bring in anything from outside. Their small stock of provisions was exhausted. Not a grain was left in their storehouse. In the absence of grain, horses, asses, and other animals were converted into food and eaten. As they had no firewood, they ate the flesh raw. Many died of dysentery and starvation.

When all grass was gone, they gathered leaves from trees. When these were all consumed, the Sikhs took off the bark of trees and broke off small shoots. They dried them, ground them, and used them in place of flour. In this way, they managed to keep body and soul together. They also collected the bones of animals, and used them in the same way. Some even cut flesh from their own thighs, roasted it, and ate it. 'In spite of all this,' writes a Muhammedan writer,' 'the Sikh Chief and his men withstood, for eight long months, all the military force that the great Mughal Empire could muster against them. None of them would even think or talk of surrender.'

But this could not continue forever. After all, they were human beings. Their continued starvation, and eating of uneatable things like grass, raw meat, leaves, bark and dry bones of animals, wrecked their physical system. Hundreds and thousands died on this account. The offensive smell of decomposed bodies of dead and dying men and animals made the place unfit for human habitation. The survivors were reduced to mere skeletons. They were half dead. They became too weak to use their swords, spears or muskets. Their magazines were empty. It became impossible for them to offer any resistance and continue the defence any longer. Still none of them thought of surrender.

48

At last, on December 17, 1715, the Sikh enclosure at Gurdas Nangal fell into the hands of the besiegers. Banda Singh and his men were made prisoners.

What happened to them afterwards, leading to their martyrdom, has been told in Book V of this series.

11

SET-BACK AND RECOVERY

The period of Sikh history from the fall of Baba Banda Singh to the permanent occupation of Lahore by the Sikhs in 1768 A.D., is full of ups and downs. It is a record of the life-and-death struggle between the Khalsa, on the one hand, and the Mughals and the Durranis, on the other. This part of Sikh history is more interesting than the history of any other people's struggle for survival and supremacy. The sons of the soil had to fight for their very lives. They had to struggle and suffer for a long time. But they did not lose heart or hope. Their sufferings served only to strengthen their resolve to carry on to a successful finish their struggle against the fanatic, foreign rule. They had to struggle long. They had to suffer terribly. They came out successful in the end. They suceeded in asserting their right to rule over their own land, to look after their own people.

After the defeat of Baba Banda Singh and the destruction of his army, there came a period of reaction and persecution. Strict measures were taken against the Sikhs. The authorities were determined not only to destroy their power, but also to uproot and finish off their community as a whole. The Mughal Emperor, Farrukh Siyar, issued an order in which it was laid down, 'An all-out campaign should be carried out against the Sikhs. They should be pursued and captured wherever found. When captured, they should be told to embrace Islam. On their refusal, they should be put to death with torture. No mercy, whatsoever should be shown to them. They have to be uprooted and finished off completely.'

50

The Emperor's orders were carried out to the letter. A reward was offered for the head of every Sikh. They were pursued and hunted and killed like wild beasts. But no Sikh agreed to give up his faith and save his life. They were, consequently, butchered most mercilessly. Farrukh Siyar had boasted that he would wipe out the name of the Sikhs from the land. Such was the keen spirit which animated his agents, that, for a time, it seemed that his boast was going to be fulfilled. Hundreds of them were caught and brought from villages. As none agreed to give up his faith, they were all executed. A reign of terror spread in the land. Thousands who had joined the Khalsa ranks merely for the sake of booty and benefits, cut off their hair, shaved their beards, and joined the Hindu flock again. The true Sikhs took shelter in jungles, hills, and deserts of Rajputana and Bikaner. Prices were laid on their heads. Whenever any of them was caught or betrayed, no mercy was shown to him. When a mother was asked how many sons she had, she would often say that she had so many (two, three, etc.), but one had become a Sikh. To be a Sikh was to be already among the dead.

This ruthless campaign was carried on vigorously for some time. But then the zeal of the Mughal official seems to have somewhat slackened. The Governor of Lahore had grown old. He had to devote his time and attention to some other risings, to tackle other problems. He could not give the same attention to the Sikhs as before. As a result, they slowly came out of their hiding places and returned to their homes and villages. They were not molested. The royal order against them came to be confined only to those who were suspected of having taken part in Baba Banda Singh's campaign. All others were left alone to pursue their peaceful callings.

At this time there set in a reaction among the Sikhs. They

51

came to be divided into opposing groups. The main clash was between the Khalsa and the Bandeis. The latter believed that Baba Banda Singh had inherited Guruship from Guru Gobind Singh. They said that Baba Banda Singh was the eleventh Guru of the Sikhs. On the other hand, the Khalsa believed that the line of personal Guruship had ended with Guru Gobind Singh; that no person could be considered to be Guru Gobind Singh's successor or the eleventh Guru. They said that he had conferred Guruship on the Sacred Granth and it was to be administered by the Khalsa. He had separated the personal and the scriptural aspect of Guruship. The one he gave to the Khalsa and the other, to the Holy Granth. Both acquired the title of Guru. They were to be addressed as Guru Granth and Guru Panth.

The Bandeis regarded Baba Banda Singh as Guru Gobind Singh's successor. On that score they claimed an equal share in the management of the Gurdwaras and the other affairs of the Panth. But the Khalsa dismissed the Bandeis' claim as wholly inadmissible.

Matters came to a head on the occasion of Diwali in 1720. Then both parties were mustered strongly at the Darbar Sahib, Amritsar. Each party tried to assert its right by a show of force. The quarrel was settled by Bhai Mani Singh. How he did it has been told in the previous book. He succeeded in bringing the Sikhs together, to make them united. All past strifes and disputes came to an end. All began to feel that they were one in the Guru. They believed that the Guru was living and moving among them. This gave them unity. This unity gave them strength and self-confidence. They began to be astir and active again. They had to move on towards their goal of liberating their country and countrymen from the grip of tyrannical, fanatic, foreign rulers.

52

12

TRAITORS PUNISHED

During the days of hardship for the Sikhs, many mean-minded people worked against them. They betrayed many of their Sikh brethren, handed them over to the Mughal officials, and earned favours and rewards. Others ill-treated their families during their exile in the hills and jungles. Still others acted as tyrants in many ways. They took possession of the exiled Sikhs' homes and lands. It was but natural for the Sikhs to cherish a longing to punish such wrong-doers.

On becoming united and strong, the Sikhs began again to bestir themselves. The first thing which the re-awakened Khalsa did, was to punish the traitors who had betrayed their brethren to the government. They also punished the mean petty tyrants who had maltreated their unprotected wives and children, and taken possession of their homes and lands.

The people thus punished would do their utmost to create mischief and involve their Sikh neighbours in trouble. It was known to all that the government was hostile towards the Sikhs. Some mean, cowardly people took advantage of the government's wrath against the Sikhs. Sometimes very petty private disputes or quarrels were given a political turn. Complaints were made to the government. It was reported that the Sikhs were persecuting loyal subjects of the Emperor; that they were punishing them for their loyalty. The Mughal authorities jumped on such complaints. They made no enquiry. They made no effort to find out the truth or to determine the nature of the alleged offence. They wasted

53

no time or thought in deciding what action would suit the occasion. They invariably took immediate and most drastic action against the Sikhs who had been pointed out by the persons complaining.

Here is an example of a petty private quarrel being made the basis of military action against the Sikhs in general. The incident occurred on the occasion of the Baisakhi festival at Amritsar.

A person named Chuhar Mal of Amritsar had two sons. One of them became a Sikh. His name was Muhkam Singh. The other remained a Hindu. He was called Ramji Mal. The latter had a fruit garden outside the city. On the fateful Baisakhi day, mulberries were being picked from the garden. A number of baskets had been filled to the brim. The picking was still going on.

A batch of half a dozen Sikhs happened to pass by the garden. They were proceeding to the Darbar Sahib in order to take part in Baisakhi celebrations. They saw the baskets full of ripe mulberries. They wanted to buy the fruit. They asked Ramji Mal's men to let them have some of it for money. Those people refused to sell the fruit to them. The Sikhs felt surprised. They said, 'We don't beg; we want to buy. After all, the fruit is meant for sale. Why don't you sell some of it to us ?'

Ramji Mal's men did not agree. They even used harsh words. The Sikhs kept cool. They took up a few handfuls of the fruit and said, 'Let us know how much we should pay. We are prepared to pay even twice or thrice the normal market price. Come, name the price.'

But Ramji Mal's men would not change their stand. They said, 'Put the fruit back in the basket and go your way. We

54

will not sell it to you.' The Sikhs replied, 'We shall pay for what we have taken. We shall not return it. Tell us what to pay.' The fruit-pickers still refused to name or accept any price. The Sikhs went away. They took away the few handfuls of the mulberries which they had taken.

Ramji Mal gave the matter a political turn. He ran to Lahore. He lodged a complaint against the Sikhs. He said, 'The Sikhs of Amritsar are out to punish all loyal subjects of the gracious Emperor. They are dead against us because of our loyal obedience to the government, and our refusal to join or side with them. They are creating trouble after trouble for your loyal subjects. They commit day-light robberies. If we protest, they attack us. We feel helpless and unsafe. We seek your protection against those lawless, law-breaking rebels and robbers. They may soon become too bold and pose a tough problem for you.'

The Lahore authorities lost no time in taking action on the complaint. A military detachment was sent to Amritsar. It was ordered to encircle the city and to punish the Sikhs in general. The military men encircled the city. Then they plundered the Sikh congregations who were engaged in Baisakhi-day celebrations. The Sikhs were obliged to fight. Soon, other parties of soldiers came from Lahore under the command of Aslam Khan. Deva, Chaudhri of Patti, and Har Sahi, his Brahmin Diwan, came with their men to help the government forces.

The siege was made closer and more vigorous. But then something happened which disheartened the besiegers. A stroke of lightning struck Har Sahi. He fell down dead. The besiegers felt terrified. The Sikhs at once fell upon the terrified enemy, and scattered them in no time. This gave rise to the famous saying:

'Harsha maria, Deva nattha, Asllan Gaee Lahore.'

*Har Sahi was killed, Deva ran away, and as for Aslan (Aslam), she went to Lahore.' (Mark here the feminine gender used for Aslam. He is called "Aslan", a feminine name, and given a feminine-gender verb.)

As a result of this incident, a police post was established at Amritsar. It was meant to keep the Sikhs in check. Their movements were watched. If they ever gathered in large numbers, they were harassed and dispersed. Even parties of Sikh pilgrims, coming to visit the sacred city, were attacked and plundered. Every effort was made to make it hot for the Sikhs. But the Sikhs did not give in. They were not overawed in the least. Their sufferings only added to their strength and determination. It made them bolder and more resolute. They challenged their persecutors to do their worst.

The Delhi government felt it necessary to take strong action against the Sikhs. It was felt that the Governor of Lahore, Abdus-Samad Khan, had become too old and weak. He was transferred to Multan. His place was taken by his more energetic son Zakariya Khan.

13

VENGEANCE

Zakariya Khan, the new Governor of Lahore, had already taken a hand in fighting and suppressing the Sikhs. He was not new to the job. By nature too, he was well suited to the cruel, inhuman task entrusted to him. He did not let the grass grow under his feet. He set about his work at once and with the utmost energy and fury. He took strong measures against the Sikhs. His aim was to root out troublesome people, once and for all. He sent out moving military columns in all directions. They were ordered to hunt out and capture the Sikhs, to tell them to choose between Islam and death, and they put to the sword all who refused to give up their faith. Prices were fixed on their heads. Every day, parties of soldiers started out from Lahore in all directions. They visited villages and forests. They captured every Sikh that they could find. The captured Sikhs were brought to Lahore in Chains. They were told to choose between Islam and death. None agreed to give up his faith. All, without any hesitation whatsoever, preferred death to a life of apostasy. They were then tortured most cruelly in different ways. Then they were beheaded in a place called the Nakhas or horse market, outside the Delhi gate. All this massacre was regarded as a *tamasha* by the 'faithful'. It was watched by thousands. To strike terror in others, the heads of the martyred Sikhs were piled up in the form of pyramids. These pyramids of Sikh martyrs' heads were called 'Shahid Gunj' or 'Martyrs' Treasure' by the Sikhs.

The Sikhs once again retired into jungles, hills, and

Persecution and killings of the Sikhs in Lahore

deserts. They lived in caves and thorny bushes. They lived on roots, fruits, green vegetables, and blades of green grass. They did not feel the least dejection or sorrow. In order to preserve their faith, they were prepared to bear manfully, even the hardest of hardship, and the cruellest of cruelties. They gave flattering names to articles of food. Layers of onions were 'silver pieces' (rupees), parched grams were 'almonds' (badam), and dry bread was a 'sweet dish' (miththa parshada). When they had nothing to eat, their kitchen was said to be 'intoxicated with abundance' (langar mastana). They were merry outlaws. They were men of unconquerable will and jovial temperament. They made fun of their misery. They would rather crow over it, and crack jokes about it.

They had been outlawed. No law protected them or their property. Anybody could plunder and kill them, without any fear of punishment. Rather, such murderers got rewards for such murders. The Sikhs, on their part, took full advantage of their outlawry. If the law did not protect them, why should they respect the law ? They had no hearths, no homes, and no property. But they did not feel disheartened or sad. They were merry and in high spirits. They fully believed that Guru Gobind Singh had prophesied that one day, the Khalsa would rule—*Raj karega khalsa*. They lived in the hope that, one day, the Guru's prophecy would come true. They waited for that happy day. Everyone of them believed 'that happy day' would come, though not necessarily during his own lifetime; he may not himself be one of the rulers. Yet every one of them lived for an idea and an ideal. He believed and hoped that the Guru's Khalsa would rule. He was most eager to contribute his best towards the achievement of that ideal. He never calculated when that happy day would come. He minded not the least if it would fail to come within his own lifetime. He toiled and suffered, nor for his own good or benefit. He was going through all that suffering and ordeal for a common cause, for the good and benefit of the Khalsa as a whole.

They were inspired by lofty ideals. All the same, they were human beings. They had human needs. They had to live. They had to keep their body and soul together. They needed food and clothes. Out of necessity, they seized food and clothing wherever they could find it. There was no alternative for them. But they took care to confine their operations to the property owned by the government, its officials, and its allies and agents. Ordinary people were not touched or troubled. If, by mistake, some innocent, harmless person's property was seized, it was restored, as soon as the mistake was discovered. The Hindus were generally spared, except, of course, those who worked against the Sikhs.

It was this time that the martyrdom of Bhai Tara Singh occurred. The story of his martyrdom has been told in the previous book. The news of Bhai Tara Singh's martyrdom stirred the Sikhs all over the Majha or Central Punjab. They vowed to wreak vengeance. They began to loot government treasures and caravans. A party was proceeding from Chawinda to Lahore, with chests of revenue-money. It was waylaid and relieved of the chests. Another similar party coming from Kasur was caught and looted. A royal merchant of Qandhar was bringing horses for the Emperor. He was attacked and deprived of his animals near Jandiala.

Because of these activities of the Sikhs, no money from revenue reached the government treasury. This continued for some years. All attempts by government forces to catch and punish the Sikh outlaws were futile. The Sikhs did not live in any house or fort. The government forces were unable to contact them. They ran away to forests or other places difficult to reach.

14

POLICY OF CONCILIATION

The young, energetic, and stony-hearted Zakariya Khan was appointed Governor of Lahore in 1726. He was assigned the task of rooting out the Sikhs from his territory called the Majha. The Sikhs of that region were most active, unbending, and troublesome. Therefore special measures were considered necessary against them. Zakariya Khan started an intensive, all-out campaign to perform the task assigned to him by the Emperor. Parties of soldiers went about, from place to place, in search of Sikhs. Captured Sikhs were brought daily to Lahore. There they were told to choose between Islam and death. Invariably, without any exception, they firmly refused to give up their faith. They cheerfully accepted death. They were subjeted to inhuman tortures and then beheaded.

This hunt and butchery went on, year after year. The Sikhs retired into forests, deserts and hills. But they did not remain idle or inactive. In order to wreak their vengeance, they began to fall upon and loot government treasures and caravans. Parties carrying revenue-money to Lahore or Delhi were waylaid and looted. For some years, no money from revenue could reach the government treasury. The forces of government tried utmost to catch and punish these outlaws. But they could not contact them.

This story of persecution and revenge went on for some years. Zakariya Khan failed to root out the Sikhs. They would constantly make their presence felt by their attacks on government treasures and on agents of the government. They simply refused to oblige Zakariya Khan by disappearing from the land or going out of existence. He felt tired of this method of dealing with the rebel outlaws. He made up his mind to change this policy. He decided to try to win them over by offering concessions and bribes.

Accordingly, in 1733, he wrote to the Emperor, 'I have tried my utmost to root out the Sikhs. Thousands of them have been put to the sword. All villages and towns have been cleared of them. But they have retired to hills and forests. Occasionally, however, they sweep down on and loot government treasures and parties carrying revenue money. As a consequence, for some years no revenue-money has reached the government treasury. All my efforts to catch these troublesome outlaws have met with failure. I have come to feel that they cannot be rooted out in this way. The more they are killed, the more they grow in numbers, and the more vigorous become their attacks. I feel almost tired. I despair of achieving success in the task assigned to me, namely, that of rooting out the Sikhs. I feel that they will have to be treated and endured as a necessary, inescapable evil. What cannot be cured, has to be endured, willy nilly. The sword has failed to crush or finish them off. Let us try if gold and favours can cool their zeal, subdue their spirits, and make them submissive. The lure of gold, favours, and power may succeed where the sword has failed. If they can be bought and won over, they will prove valuable and trustworthy allies. I would suggest that a grant be made to them, and a title be conferred on their leader. Let us try this policy of conciliation.'

The Delhi government was equally in despair in this matter. Hence, Zakariya Khan's proposal was readily accepted. He was authorised to make whatever offer he thought would be suitable. Zakariya Khan made up his plans. The next question was how to convey the offer to the Sikhs and persuade them to accept it. He looked for a suitable person who could be entrusted with the delicate, difficult task.

There was, at that time, a peaceful, obedient Sikh living in Lahore. He was a government contractor. His name was Subeg Singh. Zakariya Khan sent for him. He disclosed his plans to him. He asked him to convey his offer to the Sikhs. He urged him to use his wits and influence to persuade them to accept his offer. 'If you succeed,' added Zakariya Khan, 'you will be doing a valuable service to the government and to me in person. I shall remember it gratefully.'

Subeg Singh replied, 'Your idea is good, indeed. But the Khalsa have their own views and their own way of looking at things. It is difficult to guess what attitude they may adopt. I cannot feel sure that I shall succeed. I shall do my best, however, to bring them round, and to make them agreeable to accepting the offer.'

Accordingly, Subeg Singh went to Amritsar. The Khalsa had assembled there at the Akal Takht. He went there. He asked permission to sit in the gathering. But an objection was raised against his being permitted to sit among the Khalsa. It was said, 'The Mughal government is our mortal foe. It is out to uproot and finish us off completely. This man has been co-operating with that government. How can he be considered to be one of us ? He has acted in a manner unbecoming of a member of the Khalsa Brotherhood. He is a *tankhahia*. He has rendered himself liable to *tankhah* or penalty. He must be treated and dealt with as a *tankhahia*. He must stand up and apologize. He may sit with us after he has gone through the ceremony of *tankhah* or clearance from the blame.'

Thereupon, Subeg Singh stood up. He put a piece of cloth round his neck, stood with folded hands holding the said piece of cloth, and begged to be pardoned for his wrong acts.

The apology was accepted. He was permitted to sit in the gathering. With the Jathedar's permission, he thus addressed the assembly, 'Khalsaji, the Governor has sent me to you to make this offer on behalf of the Emperor. The Emperor offers you a jagir and the title "Nawab" to your leader. The jagir will comprise of parganas or divisions of Dipalpur, Kanganpur, and Jhabal. It will fetch an income of a lakh of rupees each year. It is a good offer. I appeal to you to accept it.'

Loud cries of 'no, no' were raised as soon as he had finished. It was said, 'It is a bait. It is a snare. The government has failed to crush us. It now wants to buy our loyalty. We refuse to sell our honour and freedom. It wants to enslave us. We refuse to be duped. Go back and tell your Governor how we react to his bait.'

Subeg Singh said, 'Khalsaji, do calmly consider this matter. Let not anger cloud your judgment. The Emperor is making the offer of his own accord. You have not begged or asked for it. He does not want you to become his slaves. You retain your honour and freedom. The only thing that he expects from you is that you stop fighting and looting. The jagir can be used for the good of the Khalsa Brotherhood. Don't throw it away.'

Subeg Singh's appeal had a good effect. Better counsels prevailed. The jagir was accepted. But no one would come forward to accept the title of Nawab and the robes of honour.

Since Baba Banda Singh's death, Diwan Darbara Singh had been regarded as the leader or Jathedar of the Khalsa. It

64

was proposed that the title and robes of honour be offered to the said Jathedar. But he would not accept them. He said, 'What is a nawabship to us? We have been promised kingdom by the Guru. The word of the Guru must be fulfilled. We need be in no hurry. The Khalsa cannot accept gifts from the Emperor. We shall rule in our own right. We shall establish our power and sway by our own strength and efforts. We cannot accept a subordinate position.

The offer was then presented to other leaders, one after another. The title and the robes were tossed about from one man to another. At last, it was suggested, in a sort of jest, that they be offered not to a leader but to a *sewadar*, someone noted for doing service to the Khalsa. Kapur Singh, a jat of Faizullapur, who used to sweep and clean the Khalsa's stables was, at that time, waving a big fan over the assembly. He was asked to accept the offer. He agreed, saying, 'I must obey the orders of the Khalsa. I accept the title and the robes of honour in obedience to the Khalsa's orders. But I shall accept them only after they have been made pure by the touch of five Khalsas' feet. Moreover, I must retain my right to serve the Khalsa, as heretofore. Even after becoming a 'Nawab', I should continue to be accepted as a *sewadar* or servant of the Khalsa, and allowed to carry on my self-chosen voluntary service of cleaning and sweeping the Khalsa's stables.'

So the title and the robes of honour were given to Kapur Singh. He became Nawab Kapur Singh. The jagir-money was duly deposited in the Guru's treasury. It was used for the good and benefit of the Khalsa, and for running a free community kitchen for all. The expenditure was controlled by prominent leaders like Diwan Darbara Singh and Nawab Kapur Singh.

15

KHALSA ARMY ORGANISED

The Sikhs were out to destroy the tyrannical, fanatical, foreign Mughal rule. They had done much to shake it to its roots. The Mughal government, on the other hand, wanted to completely root out the Sikhs in order to keep itself in power. Hence, for a long time, it followed the policy of persecuting and massacring the Sikhs. But these persecutions and murders did not succeed. They only made the Sikhs bolder, hardier, and more determined. The more they were killed, the larger grew their number. Consequently, the government got tired, of this policy. Zakariya Khan, Governor of Lahore, therefore, suggested to the Emperor that peace be made with the Sikhs. Where the sword had failed, gold and favours might succeed. In accordance with his proposal, a jagir of one lakh rupees a year was made to the Sikhs and the title of 'Nawab' was conferred on Kapur Singh.

In this way, a sort of peace was made between the Sikhs and the Mughal authorities. The Sikhs began to return from their hide-outs in the hills and forests. They began to inhabit, again, their original homes. But from the very nature of the case, this spell of peace was destined to be but short-lived. In giving them the jagir, the government had thought that the Sikhs would give up fighting and creating trouble; that they would begin to live as peaceful and law-abiding citizens. On the other hand, the Sikhs regarded this peace as only a temporary affair, a breathing time. They had tasted political liberty. They had vowed to root out the tyrannical, fanatical, foreign Mughal rule. They were dreaming of their own independent Khalsa raj. They could not remain content with the mere, empty title of 'Nawab' for their leader, and a petty jagir for the whole body of the Khalsa. They were determined to snatch power from the Mughals, and establish their own rule. They were only waiting for an opportunity to carry out their bold designs.

Hence, the Khalsa decided to use this period of peace for strengthening their organisation. As we know, since Baba Banda Singh's martyrdom, Diwan Darbara Singh had been acknowledged as Jathedar of the Khalsa. By this time their numbers had increased considerably. It was felt that it was difficult to control and manage such a large number as one group, under one leader. So, Diwan Darbara Singh took counsel with his chief companions. He wanted to improve and strengthen the organization of the Khalsa. It was decided to create two divisions of the Khalsa army. One of them consisted of old, experienced Sikhs. Many of them had seen the days of Guru Gobind Singh. They were called the Buddha Dal or the Army of Elders. They were led by Nawab Kapur Singh. Sham Singh of Naroke, Gurbakhsh Singh Roranwala, Bagh Singh Hallowalia, and Bhamma Singh were other prominent members of the Buddha Dal. The Buddha Dal had its headquarters at the Akal Takht, Amritsar. The other division of the Khalsa consisted of junior and younger men. It was called the Taruna Dal or the Army of the Young.

Diwan Darbara Singh died in 1734 A.D. By then it was found that the Young Khalsa were difficult to control in one place or under one leader. Hence, in the same year, 1734, they were divided into five Jathas. Five centres were established for them in different parts of Amritsar. These centres were at Ramsar, Bibeksar, Luchhmansar, Kaulsar, and Santokhsar.

67

Each Jatha had its own banner and drum. It comprised of 1300 to 2000 men. All the Jathas had a common mess. They also had a common store for clothing and other necessaries. Whatever was brought from outside by any Jatha, was deposited in the common treasury. All members of the Jathas were under strict discipline. No member of any Jatha could go home without leave. Both the Dals—the Buddha Dal and the Taruna Dal—were under the over-all command of Nawab Kapur Singh. They were supervised and kept together by him. Normally, the Jathas were under the command of their respective leaders. But at the time of any crisis or combined campaign, all of them were under the command of Nawab Kapur Singh, commander of the Buddha Dal.

The people of the Buddha Dal were not very active. They mostly remained at their headquarters, at the Akal Takht, Amritsar. Their aim was to keep the truce as long as possible, and to utilize the time for strengthening the Khalsa forces. But the members of the Taruna Dal were active and even on the move. They spread themselves out at first into the Bari Doab, the tract between the rivers Ravi and Beas. Then they went further afield up to Hansi and Hissar. The renewed activities of the Dal alarmed the government. The Khalsa was again in the field. The government thought that the jagir was no longer justified. It was stopped in 1735.

16

PERSECUTIONS AND RELAXATION AGAIN

Having despaired of finishing off the Sikhs with the sword, the Mughal authorities tried to buy them off, to bribe them into loyalty and peaceful obedience. But this policy of offering bribes and concession also failed. The Sikhs did not change their course. Rather they strengthened their organization in order to make it more effective.

This organization inspired a new zeal and vigour in the Sikhs. They were spurred into fresh activity. The Taruna Dal was more enthusiastic and active. This alarmed the government. It confiscated the jagir in 1735. This step was welcomed by the Khalsa. They now felt free again to deal with the government in their favourite way. The government also re-started its campaign of persecution and massacre. Lakhpat Rai, Diwan of Lahore, fell upon the Budha Dal and drove it out of Bari Doab. It came to the Malwa. There it was welcomed by Ala Singh at his capital, Barnala. With great ceremony, Ala Singh received *pahul* that is, he was baptized by Nawab Kapur Singh. With the Buddha Dal's help, Ala Singh was able to extend his territory. He annexed the whole area of Sunam.

Taking leave of Ala Singh, the Buddha Dal punished Sarhind. In that operation they acquired much 'to pay their way back to Amritsar'. Then they returned to the Majha. They wanted to celebrate the fair of Diwali at Amritsar. Passing through Goindwal and Tarn Taran, they reached Basarke, near that sacred city. While they were stationed there, they were suddenly attacked by an army of seven thousand under the command of Lakhpat Rai. The army was too strong for them. They were defeated. The Young Khalsa heard of this defeat. They hastened to assist the Army of Elders. Their combined Dals fell upon the Mughal army which was on its way to Lahore. A battle took place near Hujra Shah Muqim. The Sikhs inflicted a heavy defeat on the Mughal army. In this battle they killed a nephew of Lakhpat Rai and two important Mughal Faujdars. Emboldened by this success, the Sikhs over-ran the whole area bordering on Amritsar.

The government became upset and furious. It once again started to take strong action against the Sikhs. The sacred temple of Amritsar was taken into possession. Its approaches were picketed by military men to prevent the Sikhs from assembling there. As before, moving military columns were sent out to hunt down the Sikhs. The Chaudhries and other officials were everywhere ordered to be on the look-out for the Sikhs, to arrest them, and to send them bound to Lahore. It was further announced that anybody giving shelter or help to any Sikh would be severely punished.

The campaign of persecution and massacre was conducted with the utmost fanatic fury. Prices were fixed on Sikhs' heads. Rewards were offered for their capture and murder. The whole machinery of government, including Chaudharies and other local officials, was put into motion to crush the Sikhs. Even non-official zamindars—Hindus and Muslims— were made to lend a hand in this campaign of ruthless murder. A good many Hindus of importance, like Karma of Chhinna, Rama Randhawa of Talwandi, whole-heartedly co-operated with the tyrannical, Mughal government in this Sikh-hunting expedition. Some of them, like Sahib Rai Sandhu of Nowshera Dhala, sent cart-loads of Sikhs' heads to Lahore.

It was during this campaign that there occurred the Martyrdom of many celebrated Sikhs like Bhai Mani Singh, Bhai Taru Singh, Bhai Mehtab Singh, Sardar Subeg Singh, and Sardar Shahbaz Singh. It was also at this time that the *Chhota Ghalughara* or the Lesser Holocaust occurred. The story of all these occurrences has been given in the previous book of this series.

The Sikhs were thus passing through very hard times. Yet their spirit was not crushed or even dampened. Their persecution only served to infuse in them a firmer faith, greater zeal, and manlier courage. Not a single one of them faltered in this faith, or felt sorry for what he had to suffer on account of that faith. The sufferings they underwent together united them in bonds of brotherliness and love. A spirit of unity, a sentiment of oneness, filled them, through and through. Their bravery and splendid endurance had a wonderful effect on the people. Many courageous people joined their ranks.

On the other hand, the government again began to tire of

its campaign of persecution and murder. It was proving a failure. The Sikhs refused to be rooted out. The more they were persecuted, the bolder and more numerous did they grow. So, the government decided to relax its policy. The Sikhs normally used to gather at Amritsar twice a year, on the occasions of Baisakhi and Diwali. For some years the government had prevented them from gathering there. But then it removed the pickets. The local officials were instructed not to prevent such gatherings, as long as they were peaceful.

The Sikhs took full advantage of this relaxation in the government's policy towards them. They began to gather at Amritsar on both occasions. In such gatherings, they discussed and decided on the questions and problems facing the Panth. They also made plans for future action.

One of the problems facing them at the time, was that of adapting their organization to the needs of the time. More and more daring and adventurous Sikhs had joined the ranks of these Sikh heroes and martyrs. As time went on, more and more persons came into the field. They formed their jathas. They began to join the Dal in its bold adventures. The numerical strength of the original two Dals also increased to a large extent. It was felt that the Khalsa forces should be reorganized, so that all might work in unison for the common weal of the Panth. Accordingly, on the Diwali day of 1745, which fell on October 14, the Khalsa Army was divided into thirty jathas. The earlier division into the Buddha Dal and the Taruna Dal was suspended. Each of the thirty jathas had a prominent Sikh warrior as its Jathedar or Leader. Nawab Kapur Singh was still to be Jathedar of the Panth and of the Khalsa Army, as a whole. In their day-to-day activities, the jathas were free to act under their respective leaders. But on occasions of common danger, they all had to work under the Jathedar of the Panth

17

KHALSA DECLARED A STATE

Luckily for the Sikhs, there was then a good deal of confusion in Delhi and Lahore. The Delhi government was utterly weak. The leading nobles there were torn by mutual jealousies and strifes. Nadir Shah had dealt it a severe, staggering blow in 1739. In 1748 came Ahmad Shah Durrani. His invasion disorganized the administrative machinery of the Punjab.

The Sikhs took full advantage of the confusion reigning in Delhi and Lahore. It gave them a chance to emerge from their hide-outs and renew their activities in the Central Punjab. Ahmad Shah Durrani or Abdali had been defeated by the Mughals near Sarhind. His defeated army was fleeing towards the land from whence it had come. A band of Sikhs under Charat Singh Sukarchakia made several attacks on Durrani's fleeing followers. They pursued and pushed them to the Indus. They captured a large number of horses and a good deal of other property.

Another party of Sikhs appeared at Anandpur to celebrate Hola Mahalla. The festival occurred on March 5, 1748. After the festival, they moved towards Amritsar. Jassa Singh Ahluwala was at their head. Adeena Beg, Faujdar of Jullundur, tried to resist them. He met them at Hoshiarpur. They pushed him back and pushed on to Amritsar. Salabat Khan, officer-in-charge of the city, came out with all his force to check the Sikhs' entry. They fell upon him and

73

despatched him to the other world. They took possession of the city, as well as a large part of the district.

This event proved a landmark in the history of the Sikhs. It was the beginning of a new era for them. They did two important things immediately. The first was that they knit the scores of their scattered bands into a more homogeneous organization. In 1745 there were thirty leaders with their jathas. By 1748 their number had increased to more than twice that number. It was impossible to organise a common policy and take combined action. So it was considered necessary to bind the scores of these bands in a closer union.

As we have said before Amritsar was occupied by Jassa Singh Ahluwalia and his companions towards the middle of March 1748. The Baisakhi festival that year was to fall on March 29. It was decided to hold a Panthic gathering on that day at Amritsar. Accordingly, all Sikh leaders with their followers, met at Amritsar on March 29, 1748, the Baisakhi day. They discussed the Panthic situation. Nawab Kapur Singh proposed that there should be a single strong organization of the Panth under one supreme commander. The existence of scores of Jathas, without a common link, was a source of weakness. His proposal was accepted. The new Panthic organization was called the Dal Khalsa.

Nawab Kapur Singh had been, until then the supreme commander of the Khalsa army and Jathedar of the Khalsa Panth. He was growing old. He felt that the situation needed a younger and more energetic commander of the Khalsa forces. So he suggested that Jassa Singh Ahluwalia be chosen to take his place. He added that he himself would ever gladly and whole-heartedly co-operate with the new leader. His suggestion was accepted. Jassa Singh Ahluwalia became jathedar of the Khalsa Panth and supreme commander of the

74

Dal Khalsa. It was further agreed that he should have under him an Advisory Council of ten Sardars.

It was also declared that, henceforth, the aim of the Khalsa was to establish their own State. Thus the Khalsa was declared a State. As a step towards the achievement of that goal, eleven jathas, called Misals, were constituted, then and there. One of them was to be led by the supreme commander of the Dal Khalsa. The other ten were to be led by the ten Sardars constituting his Advisory Council. The names of the Misals were :

1. Misal Ahluwalia, led by Sardar Jassa Singh Ahluwalia, Supreme commander of the Dal Khalsa;
2. Misal Faizullapurian, led by Nawab Kapur Singh;
3. Misal Sukarchakian, led by Sardar Naudh Singh, great-grandfather of Maharaja Ranjit Singh;
4. Misal Nishan Wali, led by Sardar Dasaunda Singh, standard-bearer of the Dal Khalsa;
5. Misal Bhangian, led by Sardar Hari Singh Bhangi;
6. Misal Kanhaiyan, led by Sardar Jai Singh;
7. Misal Nakaiyan, led by Sardar Hira Singh Nakaiyee;
8. Misal Dallewali led by Sardar Gulab Singh;
9. Misal Shahidan, led by Baba Deep Singh Shahid;
10. Misal Karor Singhian, led by Sardar Karor Singh; and
11. Misal Sanghnian, led by Sardar Nand Singh. Later on, this Misal came to be called Misal Ramgarhian.

There was a twelfth Misal also. But it was not a part of the Khalsa Dal organization. It generally held aloof from the Khalsa Dal's activities. At times, it even opposed the Khalsa Dal. It was called Phulkia Misal. Its leader was Sardar Ala Singh.

The eleven Misals were formed and their formation

was announced on that Baisakhi day, birth-anniversary of the Khalsa Panth.

Then, every soldier was given the option to join which of the new jathas or misals he liked. Every Amritdhari Sikh was considered to be a member of the Dal Khalsa and on an equal status with others as a Bhai or brother. In their internal affair, all Misals were to be free and independent. But, on occasions of combined action for the good of the Panth as a whole, all the eleven Misals would be under the command of the supreme commander.

The second important thing done that day was the decision to construct a fort. The new leader, Sardar Jassa Singh Ahluwalia, said to the assembly, 'I feel that we can no longer trust our safety to bushes and caves. We should provide ourselves with a regular fort. It will serve as a base of our military operations. It will also lend security to our sacred central shrine here.' There proposal was accepted by all. A piece of land near Ramsar was selected for the purpose. A small enclosure—*rauni*—of mud walls was built there, with watch-towers at its four corners and a moat running round it. The whole work of construction was done by the Sikhs themselves. The leaders took the most prominent part in that labour of love. It could accommodate five hundred men and their horses. It was called Ram Rauni, after the name of Guru Ram Das, the founder of Amritsar.

18

RAM RAUNI BESIEGED

On the occasion of Baisakhi in 1748, the Khalsa assembled at Amritsar. Before dispersing, the Dal Khalsa made their plans for the future. They also planned spheres of action for the various groups. In accordance with those plans, the leading ·Sikhs began to assert their rule over different parts of the central Punjab. Jassa Singh Ahluwalia, Hari Singh Karoria, and others established themselves in the Bari Doab. Bagh Singh Hallowalia, Jassa Singh Ichogilia (later on called Jassa Singh Ramgarhia), and others took possession of a large part of Jullundur Doab. Charat Singh Sukarchakia established his headquarters at Gujjranwala. He spread his power over the Rachna Doab—the territory between the Ravi and Chenab.

The Sikhs were thus breaking up the Mughal State, Mir Mannu, Governor of Lahore, decided to check them. He started a ruthless campaign against them.

At times Mir Mannu himself rode out for the hunt and brought in a large bag of Sikhs. "Hundreds of Sikhs," says Syed Muhammad Latif, "were brought daily to Lahore and butchered at the *Nakhas* or Shahidganj, outside the Delhi Gate, within sight of a multitude of spectators." Finding the homes of the Sikhs depleted of men, their women and children were seized and brought to Lahore. The dark and narrow dungeons where they were imprisoned, starved, and tortured, and where little babes were cut to pieces and placed in the laps of their mothers, can still be seen in the Gurdwara Shahidganj in the Landa Bazar, Lahore. But all this persecution does not seem to have produced any effect upon the Sikhs, as is apparent from the following song of Sikh bravado coming down from those days :—

Mannu asadi datri, asin Mannude soe
Jion jion Mannu wadhda,
Asin dun swae hoe
Mannu is our sickle
And we are a crop for him to mow;
The more he cuts us, the more we grow.

Mir Mannu, at the same time, ordered Adeena Beg, Governor of the Doab, to hunt out the Sikhs in his territory. Adeena Beg was a very clever man. On the one hand, he wanted to win the good opinion of his masters by suppressing the Sikhs. On the other, he did not want to finish off the Sikhs. He feared that if he finished them off completely, there would be no need left to retain him in service. In accordane with his policy, he decided to make conciliatory gestures. He invited Jassa Singh Ahluwalia to a conference. He said to him, 'I am at heart a friend of the Sikhs. In fact, I am a sort of roundhead Sikh. I want to see the Sikhs grow and prosper. Mir Mannu has sent me orders to round up the Sikhs in my territory. You know I cannot disobey his orders. But I don't like doing what he wants me to do. I am sure, you, too, do not like the Sikhs to be cut down in the way that Mir Mannu wants. Let us stop fighting and make peace. I am making a liberal and attractive proposal. I am putting forward two alternatives. The first is that the Sikhs should rule the country jointly with me. The other is that they should accept a separate territory. For that a grant can be secured from Lahore and confirmed by the Emperor of Delhi. This arrangement will prevent much bloodshed on both sides. Let us live and rule as friends and good neighbours.'

Jassa Singh Ahluwalia replied, 'You are very wise, indeed ! You want us to accept a petty, subordinate position. You would like us to agree to rule over a small territory under the Mughals. This cannot be. The aims and outlooks of the Mughals and the Sikhs cannot be reconciled. The Mughals want to root us out. We want to destroy the foreign, fanatic and tyrannical rule of the Mughals. There can be no meeting between the parties. We shall wrest power from the Mughals by the sword, just as the Mughals did. So we can meet them only in the battle-field. You say that you want to avoid bloodshed. That may be true. But who has ever won freedom peacefully, without sacrificing the best blood of youth ? You Mughals have been hunting down and killing us like wild beasts. Now that we have taken up the sword, the Mughals have modified their position and talk of peace and friendship. When the same sword moves a little further, it will bring sovereignty to us. The Khalsa must rule in their own right, as foretold by Guru Gobind Singh, and as ordained by God. We cannot accept a subordinate position under the foreigners. We refuse to swallow this bait.'

Adeena Beg thus failed to rope in the leader of the Khalsa Dal. He turned to less important persons. He decided to try his skill with Jassa Singh Ichogilia, later on called Ramgarhia.

79

Now, Jassa Singh Ichogilia was believed to have killed his infant daughter. On that account, he was banished by the community. This enraged him. In a fit of anger he went off and readily agreed to serve under Adeena Beg. He took with him his three brothers and about a hundred followers. In his heart of hearts, however, he felt sad. His conscience smote him for having betrayed his brethren. He was ever on the lookout for a chance to go back to them. He got this opportunity during the siege of Ram Rauni.

That year (1748) the Sikhs gathered in large numbers to celebrate the Diwali festival at Amritsar. Mir Mannu got news of this gathering. He decided to fall upon them and deliver them a heavy blow. He marched with his forces to the fort of Ram Rauni. At the same time, he ordered Adeena Beg to bring up his forces. He did so. Jassa Singh Ichogilia (or Ramgarhia) and his men were in Adeena Beg's Army.

The Sikhs stood on the defensive. About five hundred of them took shelter within the fort. The rest hid themselves in the bushes near Ramsar. Those in the fort made occasional attacks on the enemy at night. The others, now and then, fell upon the enemy from outside. The besiegers had a very hard time.

The siege went on for about three months from October to December, 1748. About two hundred Sikhs inside the fort were killed. There was an acute shortage of food and fodder in the fort. Jai Singh Kanhaiya and some other daring Sikhs would, occasionally, jump over the walls, take possession of provisions from the enemy's bazar, throw them in, and climb back into the fort. But such supplies were altogether insufficient. The besieged Sikhs were in extreme distress. They said, 'Instead of dying of hunger in here, let us go out and die fighting.' Before doing so, they offered a prayer. The

80

prayer ended with an exclamation of *Sat Sri Akal*. This shout was heard by Jassa Singh Ichogilia (or Ramgarhia). It sent a thrill into his heart. He could not resist the appeal of the familiar Sikh cry. His heart told him that the Sikhs inside were about to make the supreme sacrifice. He decided to rejoin his brethren. He wrote a letter, tied it to an arrow, and sent the arrow flying into the fort. He had written, 'If the Guru Panth pardons me and agrees to take me back, I am prepared to leave the Khalsa's enemy, and join my brethren in the fort.' The Sikhs from inside sent back a letter in the same manner. It said, 'The Guru is ever ready to forgive the repentant. The Panth, too, is ready to do so. Come in, by all means. You are quite welcome.' He went in along with a hundred followers.

Just at that time the besiegers learnt that Ahmed Shah Durrani (Abdali) had entered the Punjab on his second invasion. It was in December 1748. Kaura Mal advised Mir Mannu to raise the siege of Ram Rauni and march against the Durrani invader.

Mir Mannu felt too weak to meet the invader and to continue his campaign against the Khalsa, at the same time. He got no help from Delhi. Kaura Mal advised him to make peace with the Sikhs. He accepted the advice. He allowed the Sikhs to retain their fort, Ram Rauni. He also granted them a jagir of twelve villages from the area of Patti and Jhabal. It yielded a lakh and a quarter rupees a year. This occurred in 1749.

In a few years, however, Mir Mannu's position became secure. He was no longer in need of the Sikhs' help. Again he turned into an enemy. He withdrew the grant which they had been enjoying since the early months of 1749. He started his campaign against the Sikhs again. It was even more severe than before.

19

A SIGNIFICANT CONTRAST

The Muslim rulers' policy of persecuting the Sikhs was of their usual religious policy. That policy was based on their narrow, fanatic religious beliefs. They persecuted the Sikhs mainly because the latter were not followers of the Prophet of Islam. They regarded non-Muslims as *kafirs* or worshippers of falsehood, infidels. Their religious policy was aimed at making Islam the only religion of all their subjects. Because of that religious policy, they did not spare even women and children. They believed that the greater and more cruel the tortures inflicted on the 'infidels', the greater would be the religious merit they would earn. All their inhuman cruelty was intended to please God and His Prophet, and to win them places in paradise.

You have read of the long and all-out campaign of persecution carried on by the Mughal and Afghan rulers against the Sikhs. Whenever this campaign grew too hot, the Sikhs retired into jungles, hills and deserts. Moving military columns were sent to hunt them down. Those who brought them in alive or brought their heads, were awarded prizes. The Sikhs thus captured were hammered to death with wooden clubs.

As a result of this vigorous, merciless campaign started by Mir Mannu, no men were left in the homes of the Sikhs. The Mughal forces under him seized Sikh women and children and brought them before Mir Mannu. He subjected them to cruel, inhuman tortures. He wanted to force them to give up their religion and embrace Islam. They were given very little food and water. Their children were cut into pieces before their eyes. Pieces of their children's flesh were placed in their laps or hung from their necks. They themselves were subjected to extreme physical and mental tortures. But those brave daughters of Guru Gobind Singh remained firm and unshaken. They bore all tortures most calmly, without even ever uttering a cry or groan or even a curse. They stoutly refused to yield. They preferred death to a life of apostasy. They were all killed in a most merciless manner. The incident is recounted up to this day in the daily prayers of the Sikhs. Though brutally killed over two centuries ago, they all still alive and working among us. Their example inspires us to be firm in our faith. The inspiration will continue to work for all times.

The Muhammedan invaders like Mahmud Ghaznvi, Shahab-ud-Din Ghauri, Taimur, Nadir Shah and Ahmed Shah Durrani (or Abdali), all acted in the same spirit and manner as Mir Mannu and others. They called their armies 'the armies of Islam'. Their declared purpose was *Jehad* (religious war) against *kafirs* or non-muslims. Every time they killed as many kafirs as they could. They plundered and destroyed their homes. They did not spare even their women and children. In the Great Holocaust (*Wadda Ghalughara*) of 1762, for example, Ahmed Shah Durrani butchered over eighteen thousand Sikh men, women, and children. Like all other Muslim invaders, he did all this in the belief that he was doing something most pleasing to his God and His Prophet.

Most of you must have read of how the Muslim soldiers of West Pakistan treated the Muslim and non-Muslim women and children of Bangladesh in 1971. The treatment which the invaders from the north-west, like Ahmed Shah, and their soldiers meted out to the people of India was far worse. It was fiercer, more beastly, and more inhuman. They massacred thousands and thousands. Every time they took away as many women and children as they could catch. How horrible and hair-raising must have been the sufferings of those helpless captives! The Muslim invaders and their soldiers considered all their cruelties to be so many meritorious religious acts, most pleasing to their God and His Prophet. There are some evidences to prove this.

(1)

When coming on his seventh invasion in 1764, Ahmed Shah Abdali called upon his Baloch ally, Mir Nasur Khan of Kalat, to join him in his religious war or *Jehad* against the Sikh 'infidels'. He wrote to him as follows : 'I hear that you are thinking of going on a pilgrimage to Mecca. How can you think of doing so while the cursed Sikhs are causing so much havoc ? You should march on them from there. I am marching from here. We should destroy these people, root and branch. *Be sure that a Jehad (religious war) on these infidels is more meritorious and more pleasing to our Holy Prophet than Hajj to Mecca.......... You are like a son to me and a brother in faith. Come that we may destroy these unbelievers and take away their women and children into slavery.'*

Such was the spirit which inspired the Muslim invaders and their Muslim soldiers. They had sworn to destroy the unbelievers (that is non-Muslims), and to take away their women and children into slavery. This act, they thought, was most pleasing to their Prophet. The fanatic Mughal and Afghan rulers were inspired by similar feelings and beliefs and acted in the same manner.

84

But the Sikhs behaved in an altogether different spirit and manner. They had to fight against the Muslim rulers, not because the latter were Muslims, but because they wanted to free their country and liberate its people from the grip of tyrannical, foreign rulers. They fought, not because they wanted to force their own religion on others, or to destroy those who held a different faith, but because they wanted to finish off cruel, fanatic tyrants, and end their intolerant, despotic foreign rule. They resorted to the sword after all other resources and means had been exhausted. But they did not indulge in indiscriminate slaughter. Their religion did not permit it. They fought only against those who fought against them. They fought against those also who oppressed and maltreated others. Their leaders gave them strict orders that the women and children of the enemy were not to be harmed or molested. They were not to go near the enemy's women. They were further ordered to kill only those who opposed them or had been cruel to the people. Even the Muhammedan tyrants who surrendered unconditionally, were to be spared.

They did something still more significant and praiseworthy. When Muhammedan generals came to attack them, the Sikhs would not attack or do harm to the generals' attendants and non-fighting men. If such non-fighting men fell into their hands, they allowed them to go away in safety. Here is one such instance. In 1763, Ahmed Shah Durrani despatched his general, Jahan Khan, to march against the Sikhs. The latter were led by Charat Singh Sukarchakia. He was aided by the Bhangi Sardars, Jhanda Singh and Gujjar Singh. They inflicted a crushing defeat on the Durrani's general. They forced him to hasten back to Peshawar. He had no time to take away with him all his people. A large number of his relatives and dependents fell into the hands of the Sikhs. The captured people included many women and children. What do you think the Sikhs did with them ? Did they kill them ? Did they take them into slavery ? Did they molest their women ? Surely,, the Durrani or his general would have treated his captives in some such manner. At least, the women would not have been allowed to go. But the Sikhs did nothing of the sort. They treated them kindly, like children of the common Father of all mankind. Then they sent them away safely to Jammu, well provided and under adequate protection.

Similarly, on another occasion, Ahmed Shah Durrani deputed another of his generals to punish the Sikhs. His name was Nur-ud-Din Bamezei. He too, was defeated by Sikhs led by Charat Singh Sukarchakia. With his twelve thousand men the general took shelter in the fort of Sialkot. But Charat Singh was on to him again. He was made to flee even from there. He fled in all haste to save his life. He left behind him his garrison of troops stationed in the fort. They surrendered to the Sikh Sardar. He treated them kindly. He permitted them all to go away in safety. Would the Durrani's general have behaved in the same manner if he had Charat Singh's troops in his power ? No Mughal or Afghan general had ever treated Sikh surrenderers in that way.

In fact, the Sikh generals and soldiers were always kind to such of the enemy as surrendered unconditionally. The enemy's women and children were never molested. Their religion forbade them behave that way. What a significant contrast !

(3)

'It will not be out of place to give here an estimate of the character of the Sikhs of the mid-eighteenth century from the pen of a contemporary Baluch writer. Qazi Nur Mohammed

86

of Gunjaba had accompanied Mir Naseer Khan of Baluchistan during the seventh Indian invasion of Ahmed Shah Durrani...... He spent the winter of 1764-65 in the train of the Shah and was present in all his incursion against the Sikhs "with pen in hand and sword hanging by his side." In his *Jang Namah* he has written an account of Ahmed Shah's invasion of 1764-65, and has recorded therein his own first hand impressions of the character and fighting qualities of the Sikhs. In his intense hatred for them as the opponents of the Afghan power in the Punjab, he uses all sorts of abusive language and calls them "accursed infidels", "dogs of hell" etc. But he was so deeply impressed by the lofty character and bravery of the Sikhs in their struggle for freedom that he devoted a section of his book (no. XLI, pp 156-59) *to the Bravery of the Dogs in a Religious war and in general.* Here, for once, he checks himself from calling them opprobrious names and praises them unhesitatingly. He says :— "Do not call the dogs (the Sikhs) *dogs*, because they are lions, and are courageous like lions in the field of battle.

How can a hero who roars like a lion in the field of battle be called a dog ?

If you wish to learn the art of war, come face to face with them in the field.

They will demonstrate it to you in such a way that one and all will praise them for it.

If you want to learn the science of war, O swordsmen. learn from them how to face an enemy like a hero and how to come safely out of an action. It is unjust to call them 'dog'. Truely, they are like lions in battle and they surpass Hatim (in generosity) in time of peace.

When they take the Indian sword in their hands, they

over run the country from Hind to Sind......

The body of everyone of them is like a piece of rock, and grandeur, everyone of them is more than fifty persons......

During a battle, with guns in their hands, they come jumping into the field of action, roaring like lions......

Although there are many musketeers, no one can excel them in the use of the musket. If their armies take flight, do not take it as an actual flight. It is their war of tactics......

Beware, beware of them, for a second time.

Leaving aside their mode of fighting, hear you another point in which they excel all other fighting people.

In no case would they slay a coward nor would they put an obstacle in the way of a fugitive. They do not plunder the wealth or ornaments of a woman, be she a well-to-do lady or a humble servant.

There is no adultery among these "dogs" nor are these mischievous people given to thieving......

There is no thief at all among these "dogs", nor is there any house-breaker born amongst these miscreants.

They do not make friends with adulterers and house-breakers.

They are not from amongst the Hindus.

They have a separate religion of their own."

20

LIBERATORS

The Sikhs had come to be looked upon as liberators and champions of the weak and the oppressed. They were known to be ever ready to come to the rescue of their helpless, down-trodden countrymen. They regarded such action to be their bounden duty as followers of Guru Nanak, Guru Gobind Singh. Their religion taught them to be friends of men and foes of all tyrants. Whenever, therefore, they heard that some oppressed people needed help against their oppressors, they acted at once. They rushed to their rescue. They shunned no danger, no hardships, no sacrifice. They tarried not to weigh the chances of success or failure. They cared not for their own lives. They ever considered it a privilege to die in attempting such noble rescue-campaigns. They ever remembered what their religion taught them : 'Only he should be considered to be worthy and brave, who fights for the poor and the weak; who is cut down to pieces, but never flies from the battle-field.' A few examples of such adventures are given here.

(1)

In 1738, Nadir Shah of Persia invaded India. He went through the Punjab, massacring its people mercilessly and laying waste the country-side. He plundered Delhi. He sacked the city and massacred in cold blood over a lakh of its inhabitants—men, women, and children. With elephants, camels, horses, and mules loaded with plunder, he started on his return journey. He also captured thousands of men, women and children. He was carrying them off as slaves. The Sikhs had then been forced to leave their homes and pass their days in hills, forests and the sandy deserts of Rajputana. They heard of the fate of their country's sons and daughters being driven away as Nadir Shah's captives. Their ire was aroused. They decided to release the captives. They rushed out of their hide-outs. Organizing themselves in small bands, they fell upon the rear of his army. They carried away much of his booty. They also released their country's sons and daughters from Nadir Shah's slavery, and sent them safely to their homes.

The dreaded Persian was astonished at the daring exhibited by the Sikhs. He called a halt at Lahore. He questioned Zakariya Khan, Governor of Lahore, about them. 'Whence,' demanded the imperious Nadir, 'come those long haired barbarians who dare to molest me ? Who are these mischief-makers ?' Zakariya Khan replied, 'They are a group of fakirs who visit their Guru's tank twice a year, and, after bathing in it, disappear.' 'Where do they live ? Destroy them and their homes, or they will destroy you.' 'Their homes are the saddles on their horses,' was the reply. 'Take care,' said Nadir, 'the day is not distant when these rebels will take possession of your country.' This remark of the Persian invader cut the Governor to the quick. He resolved to launch an all-out campaign against the Sikhs. But they felt no regrets at this. They had long become accustomed to the persecution campaigns of the fanatic foreign rulers. They felt sure that, one day, their persecutors would disappear from their dear Punjab.

(2)

When returning home after his fifth invasion, Ahmed Shah was taking about 2200 Hindu women and girls as

90

captives. They were to be sold into slavery in Afghanistan. On the way they were to be used by the Afghan soldiers to satisfy their lust. The Sikhs heard of this. At that time, they were, about to eat a meal. They abandoned their meal. How could they eat or drink when their countrywomen, their sisters, were in such a plight. Not caring for their lives, they rushed to do their duty as the Guru's saint soldiers. They fell upon the Afghans near Goindwal. The captive women and young girls were all released. Then they were all conducted to their respective homes in comfort and safety.

(3)

Once upon a time, Jassa Singh Ramgharia was informed that the Muhammedan official of Hissar was mercilessly persecuting the Hindus under him. He attacked the honour of their women. He had forcibly carried away two Brahmin girls. He had converted them to Islam. Jassa Singh was deeply distressed at the news. He vowed vengeance against the fanatic tyrant. He rushed to Hissar with a strong force. He fell upon the Muhammedan oppressor. He punished him. He rescued the two Brahmin girls and restored them to their parents.

(4)

On other occasion complaints were brought to Hira Singh Nakaiyee against Shekh Shujah of Pakpattan. The Hindus of that place said that the Shekh and his men were ill-treating the Hindus, dishonouring their women, and slaughtering cows in the lanes and streets. Hira Singh Nakaiyee's anger was roused. He decided to punish the cruel, fanatic Shekhs. He collected his troops and attacked the Shekhs of Pakpattan with a force of two thousand men. Unluckily, he was mortally wounded early in the engagement. He was about to die. When picked up by his companions, he heaved a sigh and said, 'I am sorry for my bad luck, my failure to rescue my oppressed countrymen and countrywomen from their oppressors. But I am glad that I am dying while attempting to do my duty. It was not my luck to succeed. I have done what I could. May His Will be done !'

He said this and his spirit flew to the feet of the Father above. His followers were disheartened. Four thousand Shekh horsemen fell upon them. They were outnumbered and over-powered. They fought heroically. They aquitted themselves admirably well as Guru Gobind Singh's lion-like warior-saints. They felt no regrets. They were glad that they were fighting for and going to die in a noble cause. They were determined to die with their faces towards the enemy. A large number of them were killed. All those heroes sacrificed their lives cheerfully while fighting for the weak and oppressed. They all became martyrs.

On one occasion, Ahmed Shah Durrani was returning from his invasion of India. He was carrying away as a prize a large number of Punjabi women and girls. His soldiers were using them as slaves. They were to be sold as slaves on reaching Ahmed Shah's country. News was brought to Jassa Singh Ahluwalia. He resolved to rescue them. He started in pursuit of the Shah. He made a night attack on his camp. He succeeded in rescuing the innocent creatures. He provided them liberally with money and other necessities. He sent them all, under proper escort, to their respective homes. From that day Jassa Singh Ahluwalia came to be called *Bandi Chhor* or Liberator. This act of bravery and patriotism endeared him to all, Hindus and Muslims alike. It increased his power and influence. It also increased the prestige and popularity of the Sikhs. They came to be regarded as defenders of the weak and the oppressed.

(5)

At another occasion the Khalsa had gathered at the Akal Takht, Amritsar, on the occasion of Baisakhi in April 1763. Some Brahmins of Kasur came. They complained bitterly against the Afghan inhabitants of their city. They said, 'The Afghans are most fanatic and cruel in their dealings with us Hindus. They slaughter cows in the streets and lanes, before the doors of our houses. They throw cows' bones into our wells and tanks. They do not allow us to perform our rites and ceremonies. If the cow of a Hindu becomes sick, the qazi goes into that house. He kills the cow there. He carries away the flesh and the skin. The hoofs, blood, intestines, and other waste parts are left there. The house-owners have to clean their house with their own hands. Yet if a Hindu does not give timely information about his dying cow, he is severely punished.'

'The Afghans freely attack the honour of our womenfolk. Nobody hears our complaints. They think they have a divine right to treat and use us as they like. The worst offender is Usman Khan. He had forcibly carried away the wife of one of us. He has converted her to Islam. We know that our Khalsa brethern are defenders of the oppressed. We have come to you for help, Khalsa ji, save us from those tyrants. Restore this Brahmin's wife to him.'

In Kasur the Afghans had a large army. They had as many as twelve forts. They were very strong. Hence, most of the Sikhs hesitated at first. They feared that the Afghans might prove too strong for them. They were in favour of sending for more saint-warriors, and awaiting their arrival. But Hari Singh Bhangi said, 'Khalsa ji, the Guru created the Panth for the sake of helping and protecting the oppressed, for relieving the helpless and the weak. So it does not become

93

the Khalsa Panth to send away disappointed any one who comes and appeals for help. We shall be failng in the duty assigned to us by the Father of Panth. We must help these helpless people. We must relieve them. We must punish the wicked evil-doers. I, for one, will go at once with all my available friends. Others may wait here as long as they think wise and proper.'

He stood up before Guru Granth Sahib, offered prayers, and begged for the Guru's and God's help for success in the undertaking. He then got ready to go. Charat Singh Sukarchakia then stood up and expressed his readiness to accompany Hari Singh Bhangi. The other leaders of the Taruna Dal followed suit.

With shouts of *Sat Sri Akal*, the Taruna Dal started towards Kasur. Sikhs in thousands joined them in the way. It was then the hot month of May. It was also the period when Muslims had to observe fasts. The Khalsa Dal reached Kasur at about mid-day. They found the city-gates open. They entered without any resistance. Because of the intense heat, the Afghans were resting and napping in their cool underground rooms. Stationing an adequate detachment to guard the gates, the Khalsa Dal fell upon the Afghans. All who resisted were put to the sword. Women and children were left unharmed and unmolested. Usman Khan, with his five hundred men were killed. The Brahmin's wife was restored to him. An Afghan chief fell at Jhanda Singh's feet. He begged for mercy. He appealed to him in the name of Guru Nanak-Guru Gobind Singh. He repented for his misdeeds. He promised to reform and behave like a good man. He begged for mercy and pardon. He offered to pay a large sum as the price of his life.

The Sikh Sardar could easily have deprived the Afghan

of all his wealth and killed him like hundreds of his cruel, wicked townsmen. But he had repented for his crimes and sins. He had promised to avoid them and lead a blameless life. Above all, he had appealed for pardon in the name of Guru Nanak-Guru Gobind Singh. No devout Sikh could ignore such an appeal. It was not the Afghan's offer of money but his appeal in the Guru's name that prevailed with that brave, devout follower of the Guru. He accepted the Afghan's prayer and spared his life.

Many more Afghans repented and promised to give up their cruel evil ways. They, too, were spared; for the Sikhs were ever averse to shedding blood unnecessarily, and they were ever ready to forgive the repentants.

The Sikhs then plundered the houses of the tyrants. The looting lasted three days. The Sikhs were amply rewarded for their pains. The Hindus of the city felt relieved. Their oppressors had been punished and made to alter their conduct towards the Sikhs.

(7)

In the course of his ninth invasion in 1767 Ahmed Shah Durrani captured about thirty thousand Hindu women and girls from Ambala and its neighbourhood. He wanted to take them to his country and sell them there into slavery. Raja Amar Singh of Patiala, son of Baba Ala Singh heard of this. He paid two lakhs rupees to the Shah and secured the release of the captives. He then arranged to send them to their homes.

(8)

When returning after his ninth invasion Ahmed Shah Durrani captured a large number of Hindu women and girls from Sialkot and its neighbourhood. Jassa Singh Ahluwalia,

Charat Singh Suakrchakia, and Baghel Singh Karorsinghia fell upon him near the banks of Jhelum. All captive women and girls were rescued. They were then conducted to their homes in comfort and safety.

(9)

In 1773 a Brahmin from Jalalabad came to the Khalsa at the Akal Takht, Amritsar. He complained that the Muhammedan official of the city, Hasan Khan, had forcibly taken away his daughter and converted her to Islam. He prayed that his daughter be rescued and restored to him. A strong Khalsa force, under the command of Kaun Singh Shahid, at once set off towards Jalalabad. Crossing the Jamna, they fell upon the city, killed Hasan Khan, and rescued the Brahmin girl. Her in-laws, at first, hesitated to accept her back. But when the Sikhs got ready to draw their swords, they agreed to take her back. The Khalsa army returned to Amritsar after having performed this duty.

Thus it was that Sikhs acted as deliverers of such of their countrymen as were maltreated or caught by the oppressors. Even Muslim victims of oppression unhesitatngly took their complaints to the Khalsa. They were all redressed without delay or discrimination. This conduct of the Sikhs brought them great credit in the eyes of the people. They began to be regarded as bold and self-sacrificing champions of the weak and down-trodden. The Muslim peasantry of the Punjab began to look upon them as brother Punjabis.

21

THE DURRANI DEFEATED

The Lahore and Delhi governments were becoming weaker and weaker. Ahmed Shah Durrani's repeated invasions were causing confusion. The Sikhs took full advantage of this situation. They took steps to extend their rule and political power. They organized a protective system of influence, called *Rakhi*. They said to Hindu and Muhammedan zamindars, 'We make you an offer of mutual benefit to us both. If you accept it, both of us stand to gain. We shall not let our men plunder you or trouble you in any way. More, we shall protect you against attacks by others. We guarantee you peace and safety. In return for such protection, you will pay us one-fifth of the annual rent of your land'.

The offer was indeed quite attractive. It provided a considerable measure of peace and safety to the persons and property of the inhabitants. It was readily accepted by most of the people in the disturbed area. A few Mughals and Muslim Rajputs, however, chose not to avail themselves of this offer. They did so on account of religious fanaticism. Some of them created trouble otherwise also. They were turned out of from their land. They had to find homes elsewhere.

In this way, the Misaldars established their control over vast areas. They set up forts in their respective territories. They began to organize some sort of government in the areas under this *Rakhi*. Thus the administration called the Misaldari system was started. Jassa Singh Ahluwalia established his rule in the Jullundur Doab. Jai Singh Kanhaya and Jassa Singh Ramgarhia brought the Riarki under their influence. The Bhangis spread themselves over parts of the Bari and Rachna Doabs. The strip of land between the Ravi and the Ghara called Nakka was under the Nakayee Sardars. The Sukarchakias occupied land around Gujjranwala. The Nishanwali and Dallewali Misals remained at Amritsar, to be available in case of need anywhere.

On the occasion of Diwali in 1760, the Misaldars or the Sardar Khalsa as they were called gathered at Amritsar. It was decided to take possession of Lahore. Accordingly, about ten thousand horsemen, under Jassa Singh Ahluwalia and other Sardars set out to attack the capital. The governor had no guts to oppose them. They were on the point of breaking into the city. At that point, prominent citizens of Lahore prevailed upon the governor to save the city by making a suitable present to the Sikhs. He made them a present of thirty thousand rupees for *karah parshad*. He begged them to spare the city. They accepted the amount and his prayer, and withdrew.

The Sikhs had, thus, brought the authorities of Lahore to their knees. Naturally, they felt emboldened. They built forts everywhere, and occupied the surrounding areas.

When Ahmed Shah Durrani was returning after his fifth invasion, the Sikhs fell upon him near Goindwal. They released about 2200 Hindu and Muslim women who were being taken as captives to Afghanistan. The retreating Afghans were attacked again and again. The Sikhs continued harassing Ahmad Shah Durrani as far as the Indus.

Returning from the Indus in May 1761, they spread themselves over most of the Punjab. Then they decided to capture Lahore. They moved up to attack the city. They

98

appeared before its walls. The leading citizens of Lahore opened the gates to the triumphant Sardars. Led by Jassa Singh Ahluwalia, they entered the capital and proclaimed him king. He coined money in the name of the Guru. The inscription on the coins was the same as Baba Banda Singh had used for his seal.

After a short time, the Sikhs broke out into the Jullundur Doab. They defeated the Durrani Faujdars. The governor of Jullundur quietly went away to the hills. Thus, the entire Punjab, from the Indus to the Satluj, passed into the Sikhs' hands.

Hearing of Sikhs' doings, Ahmed Shah Durrani came down on his sixth invasion of India. It was during this invasion that there occurred the Great Holocaust (*Wadda Ghalughara*) on February 5, 1762. The Malwa Sikhs remained peaceful. They gave no trouble to the invader and no help to their brethren in their terrible trouble. Their leader, Sardar Ala Singh of Patiala, followed a neutral policy. He gave little help or sympathy to his co-religionists in trouble. He had accepted the Durrani as his overlord. All the same, Ahmed Shah attacked his territory. Ala Singh pacified the Shah by paying him five lakhs of rupees as tribute. The Shah desired Ala Singh to appear before him with his hair cut. The latter replied that he was prepared to pay for the right to keep his hair, and for permission to appear before the Shah with his hair uncut. 'How much will you pay?' asked Ahmed Shah. 'One lakh and twenty-five thousand,' was the reply. Ahmed Shah accepted the offer. Ala Singh paid the sum. He was, thereupon permitted by the Shah to appear before him, his hair uncut.

Ahmed Shah attacked Amritsar on the eve of the Baisakhi festival, on April 10, 1762. Thousands of Sikhs had gathered there to bathe in the holy tank. Of course, they dispersed at his approach. He blew up the sacred temple with gunpowder. The *bungas*, or rest houses meant for pilgrims, were destroyed. Heads of cows were thrown into the sacred tank. It was then filled up with rubbish and refuse. As the buildings were being blown up, a brick-bat struck Ahmad Shah on the nose. It inflicted a wound from which he never recovered and which later caused his death.

The Sikhs were infuriated. In February 1762, had occurred the terrible carnage, called the Second or Great Holocaust. In April that year had occurred the pollution of their most sacred places. The two occurrences had stung them to the quick. Within four months, while Ahmed Shah was still in Lahore, they attacked Sarhind, defeated the Nawab and his Hindu Diwan, and took everything away from them.

Then large tracts were captured and occupied in various parts of the Punjab. The Sikhs even harassed Ahmed Shah. He dared not do them any harm. He simply wondered at their daring and said to himself, 'The Sikhs are strange people. I suppress them, I kill them; but they rise again. They are indeed unconquerable.'

On the occasion of the Diwali festival in 1762, 60,000 Sikhs assembled at Amritsar. They resolved to avenge the insult offered to their temple and to make up the loss of national honour suffered in the Great Holocaust. Ahmed Shah Durrani was then in Lahore. He heard of the Diwali gathering. He did not have a large enough army with him. He did not wish to meet the Sikhs on the battle-field. He wanted to avoid such a meeting. He thought of averting a clash by using diplomacy. He sent a messenger to the Khalsa. The latter was to negotiate peace with them. He was to tell them,

'You know what Ahmed Shah has done to you, what he can still do. But he does not want to shed more of your blood. He has learnt that you are planning to attack him. He has sent me to advise you against such an action. It will cause terrible bloodshed. Let us avoid it. He is eager to make peace with you. Let us sit together and draw up terms of peace !

Ahmed Shah's messenger came to the Khalsa assembled at Amritsar. He spoke to them as he had been told to do. But the Sikhs were in no mood to listen. They saw through the Shah's trick. They did not let the messenger finish his speech. They did not listen to his proposals. They plundered him and his followers, and drove them away. They said to him, 'Tell your master that this is how we shall deal with him.'

Ahmed Shah Abdali's efforts at 'peace' thus proved unavailing. He felt insulted. He was enraged. He marched from Lahore and reached Amritsar on October 16, 1762, the day before Diwali. Early next morning, after saying their prayers, the Sikhs made a desperate attack on the enemy. Shouts of *Sat Sri Akal* rent the air. The Durrani forces were struck with terror. 'He was compelled to withdraw his forces and escape to Lahore under cover of darkness. The skill of the greatest military genius of the time in Asia gave way before the zeal and determination of the Sikhs born of religious fervour and sacrifice.' He left Lahore for Afghanistan on December 12, 1762.

Soon thereafter, the Khalsa assembled at Amritsar. The Dal Khalsa was re-organized. It was divided once more into two Dals—the Buddha Dal and the Taruna Dal. The Buddha Dal comprised of six Misals : Ahluwalia, Singhpuria, Dallewalia, Karor Singhia, Nishan Walia, and Shahidan. The leader was Jassa Singh Ahluwalia. It was assigned the task of making conquests and punishing the Khalsa's enemies. The Taruna Dal comprised of five Misals : Bhangi, Ramgarhia, Kanhaiya, Nakayee and Sukarchakia. Hari Singh Bhangi was to be its leader. It was assigned the duty of serving and looking after the sacred places at Amritsar. It undertook to cleanse the holy tank and rebuild the ruined temple. When the occasion arose, the Taruna Dal also issued forth to make fresh conquests.

Thereafter the Sikhs made more conquests, and acquired more territories. Then they turned to Malerkotla to punish its governor, Bhikhan Khan, for the part he had played in the Great Holocaust. He was defeated and killed. In this battle Ala Singh of Patiala also sent his contingent to help the Buddha Dal, though before he had given no help or shelter to the Sikhs involved in the Great Holocaust.

The Dal then moved on in a north-easterly direction and fell upon Morinda. Two Muslim inhabitants of that place had arrested Guru Gobind Singh's mother and his two younger sons. They had then handed them over to the Nawab of Sarhind who had them killed in 1704.

22

FRESH CONQUESTS AND MORE SUFFERINGS

After dealing with Morinda, the Sikhs turned to Sarhind. Its faujdar, Zain Khan, had become very unpopular on account of his high-handed rule.

The two Khalsa Dals, under the command of Jassa Singh Ahluwalia, made a determined attack on Sarhind in January 1764. They were helped by Ala Singh's Patiala contingent under the command of Himmat Singh and Chain Singh. The governor tried to run away. He was shot dead. His troops fled in panic in all directions. The city was plundered. Its buildings were razed to the ground. Afterwards, the place was ploughed over using donkeys. That was done in order to fulfil a popular prophecy. The spot where the infant sons of Guru Gobind Singh had been bricked up alive and killed, was sought out. A Gurdwara, called Fatehgarh Sahib (or Fort of Victory), was built on it.

With this victory the whole country from the Satluj to the Jamna, fell into the hands of the Sikhs. It was partitioned by the chiefs among themselves. The method adopted by them to mark out villages and towns as theirs, was unique, original and interesting. As soon as the battle was over, horsemen galloped off in various directions. In each village or town that a horseman visited, he threw down some article of his—belt, scabbard, stick, pieces of dress etc. This he did in order to mark the place as his. He went on doing so day and night, until he was almost naked. All villages and towns into which he threw his articles became his.

Those horsemen would first demand money from the Zamindars of the villages through which they passed. If no money was forthcoming, they would ask for some *gur* (coarse sugar). If even that was not available, they would take some loaves of bread. They would then depart and visit other places. The villagers felt amused at all this. They took it as a mere joke. But the Sikh horseman soon returned. Taking these petty offers as the tokens of the villagers' submission, he would establish his sway over every village through which he had ridden.

The country around Sarhind was thus partitioned and occupied. But no one came forward to accept the city of Sarhind. It was regarded as being of accursed memory. Thereupon, the leading residents of the city were invited to choose their own master. They declared themselves in favour of one Bhai Budha Singh, an old companion of Guru Gobind Singh. From him Baba Ala Singh later purchased it for the sum of Rs. 25,000.

After conquering Sarhind, the two Dals separated and started on fresh conquests. The Buddha Dal crossed the Jamna and conquered a good many places in the Gangetic Doab. The Taruna Dal conquered the Jullundur Doab and partitioned it among themselves. Then they pushed on to Lahore. They seized the neighbouring country. In February 1764 they threatened the city itself. At that time the governor of Lahore was Raja Kabuli Mal. He held that post under Ahmed Shah Durrani. The Sikhs sent to him the following message : 'We have learnt with pain and surprise that cows are being freely killed in the city under your rule. You are Hindu. How can you allow cow-slaughter under your very eyes ? It is a matter of shame for you. What is still worse, the butchers have grown so bold that they slaughter cows publicly. Only recently a batch of them killed thirty cows in a public place. We wonder how you can tolerate all this ! We cannot let things go on that way. We call upon you to hand over all those butchers to us. More, you must prohibit cow-slaughter altogether in future. If you do not agree to all this, we shall attack and take the city. Make your choice without delay.'

The Hindu governor replied, 'Khalsa ji, I am a servant of a Muslim King. I cannot do anything which my master will not allow. I cannot prohibit cow-slaughter. If I try, I shall be involved in trouble with my master, the Durrani King. I am helpless.'

On getting this reply, the Sikhs fell upon the city. They broke through the Delhi Gate. They went on advancing rapidly. Kabuli Mal was terrified. He decided to yield. With the consent of leading citizens, he cut the hands and noses of a few butchers. He appealed to the Sikhs to accept that action as sufficient and satisfactory. He paid a large sum to the Taruna Dal. He also agreed to keep with him an agent of Hari Singh Bhangi to direct him in the work of administration. A Munshi of Sobha Singh sat with the Afghan officials at the Shah Almi Gate and received a fixed share of the custom on his behalf.

The Taruna Dal was then divided into two sections. One section, under Hari Singh Bhangi, marched to the south-east. The other, under Charat Singh Sukarchakia took to the north-west. The former conquered the whole region called Lamma and Nakka and gave it to the Bhangis. Then they crossed the Indus and occupied the territories of the Derajat.

The other division of the Taruna Dal marched across the Rachna and Chaj Doabs, and captured Rohtas. The regions of Dhani, Pothohar, Chakwal, and Pind Dadan Khan were conquered next.

Ahmed Shah heard of the Sikh's activities. He came down again to India. It was his seventh invasion. He acrossed the Indus in October 1764, with a horde of 18,000 Afghans. He was joined by 12,000 Baluchis. Thousands more, eager to kill and plunder the *Kafirs* joined him to the way. All these, about thirty six in number were *Ghazis—* soldiers of God engaged in a regligious war. At Lahore Raja Kabuli Mal joined his camp. He remained with the Shah throughout his ferocious campaign against the 'infidels.'

The Sikhs left their places on the Grand Trunk Road and vanished out of sight. They retired into the Lakhi jungle. But they made their presence felt now and then. They would suddenly fall upon the enemy and inflict heavy losses. Ahmed Shah left powerless to check them. In anger, he resolved to attack Amritsar and level it to the ground. He had done so several times before. But the Sikhs had risen every time and rebuilt their holy place. He reached Amritsar on December 1, 1764. He had been told that a large number of Sikhs would be found there. But he did not find any Sikhs there except a few that had been left in charge of the Akal Takht. They were only thirty in number. But they did not have a grain of fear about them. They considered themselves to be thirty lakhs.. They were resolved to sacrifice their lives for the Guru. They were determined to die fighting in defence of their sacred place. They acted gloriously. The *Ghazis* far out-numbered them. But every one of them grappled with the attackers, killed many, and then achieved martyrdom. Their leader was Gurbakhsh Singh Shahid. His Shahidganj stands behind the Akal Takht.

The Shah's men then ran right and left in search of more Sikhs. They could find none. The Shah was angry and disappointed. He destroyed the sacred buildings and returned to Lahore. They must have been in high spirits over their

106

wonderful performance ! Had not they, a few thousand in number, put to the sword as many Sikhs as, in the Khalsa vocabulary, numbered no less than thirty lakhs ? A memorable victory, indeed !

This historic incident is described by an eye-witness, Gazi Nur Muhammed, in his book named *Jang Namah*, in the following words :—

'When the Shah arrived at the Chakk (Amritsar), and entered the Darbar Sahib on December 1, 1764, there was not a single *kafir* (Sikh) to be seen there. But a few of them had remained in an enclosure (the *Bunga* of the Akal Takht) so that they might spill their own blood. And they sacrificed their lives for the Guru. When they saw the renowned king (Ahmed Shah Durrani) and the army of Islam (numbering about thirty six thousand), they all came out of the enclosure. They were only thirty in number. They had not a grain of fear in them. They had neither the fear of slaughter, nor the dread of death '

'Thus (unmindful of the overwhelming strength of the Shah's army—36 thousand against thirty), they grappled with *Ghazis* and in the grappling they spilled their own blood. All of them were killed.'

Ahmed Shah Durrani then decided to move his armies towards Sarhind. He chose the pass through the Riarki and Doaba. They were homelands of the Sikhs. He wanted to plunder and ruin them. He allowed his soldiers to plunder the territory to their hearts' content. And they did so mercilessly. Thousands were massacred in broad daylight. They did all this to punish the 'Kafirs' and to please their own God and His Prophet.

On reaching Sarhind, Ahmed Shah found the city in

ruins. He was shocked to see the sight of destruction. That city was in the territory of Patiala. Ala Singh of Patiala regarded Ahmed Shah Durrani as his king and lord. He came to meet and pay respects to the Shah. The latter enquired from him how the once magnificent city of Sarhind had come to be in that condition. Ala Singh replied, 'It has been destroyed by the Sikhs. They are most incorrigible. I have tried to dissuade them. I have fought and punished them, a number of times. But they do not care. They refuse to mend their ways. People go on joining their ranks in ever increasing numbers. If one of them dies, two more come forward to take his place. Such is the boon granted to them by their Guru. Moreover, they hate Sarhind. If your Majesty were pleased to confer the territory of Sarhind on me, I shall soon re-populate it better than ever before.'

Ahmed Shah accepted Ala Singh's prayer. He granted him the title of Raja. He bestowed on him a drum and banner. Raja Ala Singh promised to pay an annual tribute to three and half lakh.

The Durrani wanted that the other Sikh chiefs to follow Ala Singh's example. But they were not at all inclined to accept kingship from the hands of a foreigner. Ahmed Shah Durrani was more hateful to them than a mere foreigner would have been. He had dishonoured and destroyed their sacred places. He had killed thousands and thousands of their men, women, and children. How could they agree to be under him ? How could they make friends with him ? They preferred to continue the struggle and win real freedom and power. They even punished Ala Singh for having submitted to the hated foreigner.

23

FINAL OCCUPATION OF LAHORE

Ahmed Shah Durrani came to India in October 1764 on his seventh invasion. He departed homewards at the end of March 1765. As usual, the Sikhs pursued him at a distance. They fell upon his camp, now and then, and took away much booty every time. They also released from captivity a large number of men, women, and girls. The Durrani gnashed his teeth in impotent rage and marched on.

The Sikhs assembled at Amritsar to celebrate the Baisakhi festival of the year 1765. On that Baisakhi day they decided by a *gurmata* to take possession of Lahore. Accordingly, the Bhangi sardars, Lehna Singh and Gujjar Singh, with two thousand troops approached Lahore. They encamped at Baghbanpura. They won over a few *Arains* (Muslim gardeners) of that place who worked as gardeners in the Lahore fort. The *thanedar* (commander) of the fort was also won over. At a place suggested by them, a hole was made in the wall of the fort. Through that hole Gujjar Singh entered the fort with fifty chosen warriors. Then, at a given signal, Lehna Singh rushed into the fort with the whole Khalsa army.

Raja Kabuli Mal, governor of Lahore, was away. Very little resistance was offered by the garrison. After prayers and amid shouts of *Sat Sri Akal*, the Khalsa flag was planted on the fort. Early next morning Sobha Singh Bhangi also joined the above two Bhangi sardars. The city and the country around it were divided among themselves by the three sardars—Lehna Singh, Gujjar Singh, and Sobha Singh.

With this conquest, the whole country between the Jhelum and the Jamna passed into the hands of the Sikhs. They looked upon this achievement as the mark of the Guru's special favour. Therefore, when they coined money, they put on their coins the same Persian inscription which had already appeared on the seals of Baba Banda Singh and the coins of Jassa Singh Ahluwalia :—

'Deg o tegh o fateh o nusrat be-dirang
Yaft az Nanak Guru Gobind Singh.'

Its English translation would be :—

'The Kettle and the Sword (symbols of Charity and Power), Victory and ready Patronage have been received from Guru Nanak-Gobind Singh.'

The coins were popularly known as 'Nanak Shahi' coins. Now the Punjab was the richest province in Ahmed Shah Durrani's dominions. The Sikhs had taken possession of it. They had become masters of the country from the Jamna to the Jhelum. Naturally, the Shah did not like the loss of his richest province. He wanted to recover it. But for two years he did nothing. Then in 1767 he came down again on the plains of India. His object was to make a final effort to recover the Punjab.

But he was growing old. As we know, in 1762 he had received a wound on the nose at Amritsar. The sacred buildings there were being blown up. A brickbat struck him on the nose. That wound developed into cancer. Hence, besides being old, he was suffering from cancer of the nose. The Sikhs were well established in the Punjab. It was no easy

110

matter to dispossess them of the province. There was no chance, therefore, of his recovering the Punjab by force of arms. Consequently, he tried to preserve his sway by following a policy of conciliation. He said to himself, 'I shall try to persuade some strong Sikh Sardar to accept governorship of Lahore from me. He will be under me. He will pay me tribute like Ala Singh of Patiala. In that way, my sway over the Punjab will be preserved.

On reaching Lahore, he found that the Sikh rulers of Lahore, (Lehna Singh, Gujjar Singh, and Sobha Singh) had left the city. Of course, they intended to come back as soon as he had gone back to his country. He did not know what to do; whom to choose as governor of Lahore. At that time a deputation of Lahore citizens came to wait upon him. It consisted of prominent Hindus and Muhammedans. They said to him, 'Since 1765 the city had been governed by three Sikh Sardars. One of them was Sardar Lehna Singh. He was a very good and sympathetic ruler. He was just and kind to all. He made no distinction between Sikhs, Hindus, and Muhammedans. He treated them all alike. All were free to live, pray and worship in their own way. On the day of Id, he bestowed turbans on the Qazi, the Mufti, and the Imams of the mosques. He was justly popular among all—Hindus and Muhammedans alike. All were happy under his rule. If your Majesty be pleased to appoint him our governor, the citizens will feel happy and grateful. If anyone else is appointed, he is sure to be turned down by the Sikhs.'

On hearing this, the Shah said, 'I am very sorry that such a good and popular ruler should have fled away. I would have gladly confirmed him as governor of Lahore. I shall be glad if he were to return and become your governor. I shall try to prevail upon him to do so.'

Accordingly, he wrote to Lehna Singh. He offered him governorship of Lahore with great honours. But Lehna Singh was made of sterner stuff than the Shah had thought. He declined the offer. He said, 'How can I accept any gift or favour from you ? How can I forget the huge wrongs that you have done to my country and my countrymen ? You have, again and again, plundered my country. You have murdered thousands over thousands of my countrymen—men, women and children. You have driven away thousands to them to your own country and sold them there into slavery. You have again and again, dishonoured and destroyed our sacred places. How can we forget all these wrongs ? How can I agree to be friends with you ? How can I agree to accept a post under you ? The Khalsa will rule and land in their own right. We shall occupy Lahore as soon as you leave, and turn out the governor appointed by you.'

Ahmed Shah was disappointed. His choice fell on one Dadan Khan knowing fully well that it is a temporary affair.

As soon as he crossed the Indus, the Sikhs, under Charat Singh and others, stormed the fort of Rohtas. They turned out its Durrani governor. The three joint rulers of Lahore occupied the city again. The fall of Rohtas extended the Khalsa dominions to the banks of the Indus. Thus, in 1768, the Khalsa commonwealth extended from the Jamna to the Indus. The Khalsa thus became the paramount power in the Punjab.

But their rule was not at all communal. All Punjabis— Hindus, Sikhs, and Muslims—were treated alike; all received equal justice and protection. In fact, all Punjabis came to realize the difference between the previous Mughal and Afghan rule and the newly established 'Khalsa rule.' They felt that they were being governed by their own people, fellow-Punjabis, whose interests were common with them. The Khalsa rule was thus the Punjabis' rule in the Punjab.